TRACKSIDE
ON THE

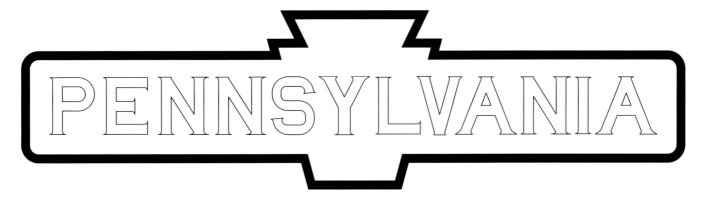

STANDARD PLANS
OF THE
STANDARD RAILROAD OF THE WORLD

JEFF SCHERB

HIGHLANDS STATION, INC.
AURORA, COLORADO

Library of Congress Card No. 2002113936
ISBN 0-9655365-5-6
First Edition
First Printing, October 2002

TRACKSIDE
ON THE

CONTENTS

INTRODUCTION

FOUNDED IN 1846, the Pennsylvania had become one of the largest industrial enterprises in the world by the early part of the last century. In 1880, the Pennsylvania was the world's largest corporation, with 30,000 employees and $400 million in capital (about $7 billion in today's dollars). In the 1920s, the Pennsylvania Railroad's trackage peaked at 11,551 miles, and the railroad moved 1/20th of the world's freight commerce. In 1939 the railroad rostered 4,753 steam locomotives, 6,499 passenger cars and 238,101 freight cars, which represented 10.6 percent of all locomotives, 16.2 percent of all passenger cars and 13.4 percent of all freight cars on American railroads.

The Pennsylvania physical plant also had numerous "biggests" — the Hell Gate Bridge was the longest arch bridge in the world at the time of its construction; the Rockville Bridge across the Susquehanna was the largest masonry arch bridge in the world; the Sunnyside Yard outside of Manhattan was the largest passenger yard in the world — and the list could go on.

Many of these "biggests" were achieved during Pennsylvania president Alexander Johnson Cassatt's capital expansion program, which began in 1900. Widely regarded as being responsible for many of the Pennsylvania's monumental achievements, Cassatt was also responsible for many of its smallest, through his drive for standardization.

Alexander Cassatt began the standardization program on the Pennsylvania in 1867. Working his way up the ranks like most Pennsylvania executives, Cassatt became Superintendent of Machinery and Motive Power in that year, and implemented the standardization of locomotive classes. Standard locomotives were designed for specific purposes, and as much as possible, parts and equipment were interchangeable between the classes to further reduce maintenance and repair costs. Between 1867 and 1872, the first eight standard classes of locomotives were developed. By 1873, 373 out of the 916 locomotives in service belonged to one of these standard classes, and by 1876, more than half of all Pennsylvania locomotives were standardized.

Cassatt was also responsible for many of the firsts on the Pennsylvania. He pioneered the use of the Janney coupler in 1877. This coupler was adopted in 1882, and Janney variants remain the standard coupler on all North American railroads even today. Cassatt worked with Westinghouse in the development of air brakes, and by July 1879, all Pennsylvania passenger equipment was so equipped.

Frank Thomson became president of the railroad in January 1897, and his three-year term in that office isn't notable except that he continued the standardization program and pushed the standardization of design and construction materials to all aspects of the physical plant. Succeeded in 1899 by Alexander Cassatt, the standardization efforts continued and were in part responsible for the "Standard Railroad of the World" slogan.

The standard locomotive and rolling stock designs of the Pennsylvania are well known and well documented in both the prototype and model railroad press. Complete volumes have been devoted to the 425 standard K-4 4-6-2 Pacific and 598 standard I-1 2-10-0 Decapod locomotives, and volumes have also been devoted to Pennsylvania hopper cars and passenger equipment.

The subjects of this book are things that were much more common than any of the aforementioned, but perhaps because of their routine and ordinary nature, have received very little historical coverage.

The goal of this volume is to document many of the standard small structures, bridges, signals and signs to be found trackside on the Pennsylvania. For the model railroader, this volume provides a wealth of information enabling the creation of a prototypical and well-detailed right-of-way. A fully detailed right-of-way can add a great deal of realism and richness to the scene and to model railroad operations. Most of these items are also simple modeling projects, and many can fit into the "one evening" category. For the prototype enthusiast or historian, this volume should provide a look into an aspect of the Pennsylvania that is rarely covered. ▼

STRUCTURES

P.R.R. STANDARD STRUCTURES

THE PENNSYLVANIA WAS KNOWN for some of the most impressive and imposing structures created by a business enterprise. Probably the most impressive was New York City's Pennsylvania Station. With its main building occupying 7.5 acres and costing $112 million (about $2 billion in today's dollars), the station opened in 1910 and served until 1963, when it was demolished. The demolition of such a grand structure caused such an uproar that it became the catalyst for the historic preservation movement in this country.

Even though Pennsylvania Station was torn down, many other examples of Pennsylvania architecture and grandeur remain. Philadelphia's 30th Street Station, completely restored in the 1990s, is perhaps the greatest remaining example. The Pennsylvania also participated in many of the great Union Stations of the period, including Washington, D.C., which has also been restored to its former grandeur.

For every one of these impressive monuments to the power of the Pennsylvania, on every mainline and branchline there were literally hundreds of smaller, less impressive, but no less important or functional structures. These structures were found at frequent intervals along the line — maintenance-of-way requirements dictated frequent tool house placement so that tools and supplies could be readily available when and where needed, the block and interlocking system required signal cabins and block operator cabins usually at five-mile intervals, and passenger shelters would be located anywhere revenue passengers were likely to be found in quantities insufficient to justify a full station.

The frequency of these structures, and their size and simplicity make them excellent subjects for the model railroad right-of-way. Even with the compressed distances required on a model railroad, quite a few of these structures could be used on the typical layout.

A 1911 Standard Plan (p. 8) describes two types of passenger shelters — one for "important stations," and one for "unimportant" stations. It would seem that both types would be for unimportant locations, since by definition the location did not qualify for a full station structure, but nevertheless the "important" passenger shelter plan called for a concrete foundation and a slate roof while the "unimportant" shelter had a gravel floor and "Ruberoid" roofing.

Watch Boxes were placed at grade crossings until automatic block detection and crossing gates became common toward the middle of the last century. Crossing watchmen operated the manual crossing gates and used a Stop Sign (p. 91) to control traffic at the crossing. Watchmen were also required to inspect passing trains for hot boxes or other defects, and according to the *Pennsylvania Book of Rules* for 1925, were required to report engineers who failed to properly sound the whistle or ring the bell at the crossing, and were to keep the crossing area clear of snow or other debris that might interfere with safe operation.

Tool Houses were one of the most common structures seen trackside in the early half of the last century, typically spaced between five and ten miles apart along the track. Track Foremen were given one or more sections of track to maintain, and were responsible for turnout maintenance, replacement of broken ties, leveling of track joints, tightening of track bolts and other general maintenance tasks along the right-of-way. By the late 1930s, economics and improvements in track maintenance equipment caused an increase in track mileage assigned to each track foreman, and tool houses began to disappear.

Signal cabins varied in design by time period and purpose. The earlier cabins were ornate designs with Victorian details, such as found on the Octagonal Signal Cabin (p. 13) used at block boundaries. The size of signal cabins that controlled interlockings was based on the size of the Union Switch & Signal interlocking machine to be installed inside. In later years, signal cabins were of brick construction (p. 15). The Pennsylvania's Zoo Tower in Philadelphia is said to have been the largest interlocking in the world, but there were many smaller structures of similar design. By 2001, less than 120 interlocking towers were in operation on all railroads in the United States, having been made obsolete by computerized interlocking and CTC systems.

Many of the early signal cabins also served as train order stations. A semaphore (p. 14) placed on or near the structure indicated to the engineer that he was to stop at the signal cabin and pick up Train Orders.

Telephones, either in Telephone Booth structures or in simpler Telephone Boxes, were placed wherever there was a need for an engineer or conductor to talk to the dispatcher or block controller. Block Limit Stations (see Signs p. 73) were accompanied by a telephone because the train was required to stop at these signals unless permitted to continue without stopping by a Train Order. Without the specific authority of a Train Order to the contrary, the engineer was required to call ahead for clearance to proceed.

Scale Houses (p. 19) were most often situated at yard throats or on the outskirts of a yard so that loaded cars could be weighed on their way out. They were also found at points where bulk shipments originated, such as large breweries, grain elevators and coal yards. Sometimes large bulk shippers such as gravel, sand or stone quarries would have a scale on site, and they could often be found at points where branchlines joined the mainline.

According to *The Keystone*, the publication of the Pennsylvania Railroad Technical and Historical Society, stations and other trackside structures were painted PRR Standard Buff with Standard Brown Trim. The Society has published the following formulas for these colors using Floquil paint — Standard Buff: 3/4 ounce #11 Reefer White, six eyedroppers #70 Roof Brown, three eyedroppers #87 Depot Buff. Standard Brown: 3/4 ounce #70 Roof Brown, five eyedroppers #11 Reefer White. *The Keystone* says, "the formulas are slightly darker than the paint chips so the desired aging effect can be achieved."

Steam engines, thirsty for water to make steam, required frequent stops. While an engine could often make its entire run with one load of coal, it was much less likely to do so on a single tender of water, so water tanks were typically spaced every 15-30 miles along the line. Almost all places where an engine would routinely stop, such as a station, had a water tank. Tanks were also placed at places where locomotives used a lot of steam, such as at the top of a long grade.

The earliest tanks were square affairs of wooden construction, but by the 1860s round wooden tanks became standard. Wooden tanks were easily constructed by carpentry crews and were inexpensive. The poor heat conducting qualities of wood also helped prevent tank freezing in the winter. The earliest round wooden tanks were tapered, getting larger near the bottom, which allowed the use of pre-riveted staves to be hammered down the taper until tight. Later, with the use of turnbuckles, the tanks had straight sides. The life of a wooden tank was typically 20 years.

Where water was plentiful, such as in or near cities, tanks could be smaller because they were easily filled, but larger tanks were used in locations where water was harder to come by. Wherever possible, larger tanks were used because a third shift pump house operator could be eliminated on busier lines.

Steel water tanks began to be used in the early teens. As steam engines grew larger and more powerful, their demand for water increased, so by the 1920s, many railroads were replacing smaller wooden tanks with all-steel designs. Often these larger-capacity tanks were positioned away from the tracks, so water was supplied to locomotives via standpipes, which could be erected where they were needed most. Many of these steel tanks lasted beyond the days of steam and still supply water to shops or other company facilities. ▉

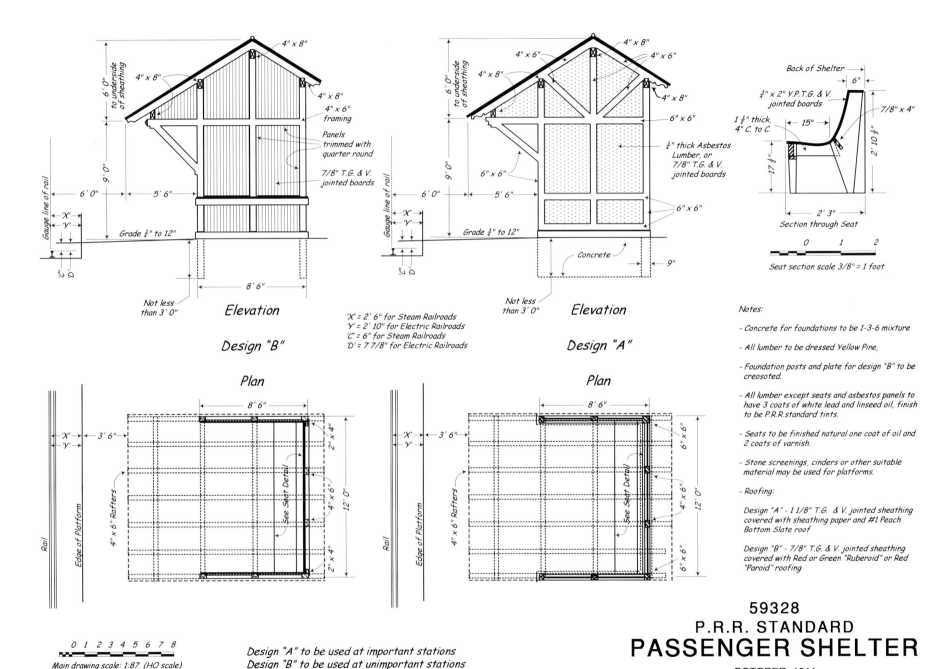

Elevation

Design "B"

4" x 8"
4" x 8"
4" x 8"
4" x 6" framing
Panels trimmed with quarter round
7/8" T.G. & V. jointed boards
6' 0" to underside of sheathing
9' 0"
Gauge line of rail
6' 0"
5' 6"
'X'
'Y'
Grade 1/4" to 12"
'C' 'D'
Not less than 3' 0"
8' 6"

Elevation

Design "A"

4" x 8"
4" x 6"
4" x 6"
4" x 6"
4" x 8"
6" x 6"
6" x 6"
6" x 6"
1/4" thick Asbestos Lumber, or 7/8" T.G. & V. jointed boards
6' 0" to underside of sheathing
9' 0"
Gauge line of rail
6' 0"
5' 6"
'X'
'Y'
Grade 1/4" to 12"
'C' 'D'
Not less than 3' 0"
Concrete
9"
8' 6"

'X' = 2' 6" for Steam Railroads
'Y' = 2' 10" for Electric Railroads
'C' = 6" for Steam Railroads
'D' = 7 7/8" for Electric Railroads

Section through Seat

Back of Shelter
6"
4 3/4" x 2" Y.P.T.G. & V. jointed boards
7/8" x 4"
1 1/2" thick, 4" C. to C.
15"
17 1/2"
2' 10 1/2"
2' 3"

Seat section scale 3/8" = 1 foot

0 1 2

Plan

8' 6"
2" x 4"
4" x 6"
2" x 4"
12' 0"
'X'
'Y'
3' 6"
4" x 6" Rafters
Rail
Edge of Platform
See Seat Detail

Plan

8' 6"
6" x 6"
4" x 6"
6" x 6"
12' 0"
'X'
'Y'
3' 6"
4" x 6" Rafters
Rail
Edge of Platform
See Seat Detail

Notes:

- Concrete for foundations to be 1-3-6 mixture

- All lumber to be dressed Yellow Pine,

- Foundation posts and plate for design "B" to be creosoted.

- All lumber except seats and asbestos panels to have 3 coats of white lead and linseed oil, finish to be P.R.R. standard tints.

- Seats to be finished natural one coat of oil and 2 coats of varnish.

- Stone screenings, cinders or other suitable material may be used for platforms.

- Roofing:

Design "A" - 1 1/8" T.G. & V. jointed sheathing covered with sheathing paper and #1 Peach Bottom Slate roof

Design "B" - 7/8" T.G. & V. jointed sheathing covered with Red or Green "Ruberoid" or Red "Paroid" roofing

0 1 2 3 4 5 6 7 8
Main drawing scale: 1:87 (HO scale)

Design "A" to be used at important stations
Design "B" to be used at unimportant stations

59328
P.R.R. STANDARD
PASSENGER SHELTER
OCTOBER, 1911
Redrawn from original PRR drawings by Jeff Scherb

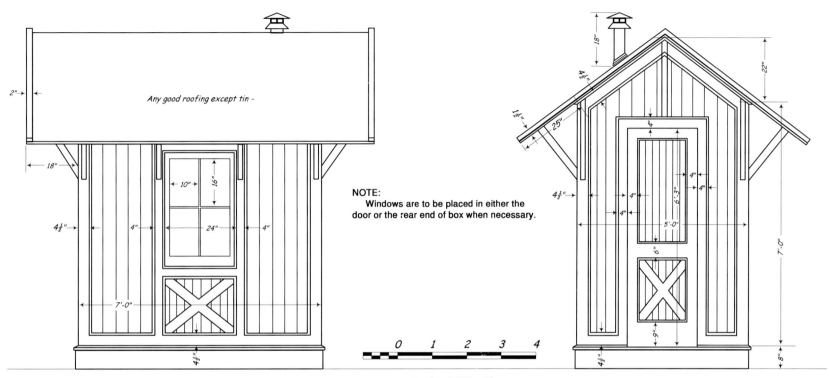

Any good roofing except tin –

2"

18"

10"

16"

4"

24"

4"

4½"

7'-0"

4½"

18"

22"

4½"

1½"

25"

4"

4"

4"

4"

6'-3"

5'-0"

6"

9"

7'-0"

8"

4½"

NOTE:

Windows are to be placed in either the door or the rear end of box when necessary.

0   1   2   3   4

Scale: 3/8" = 1'

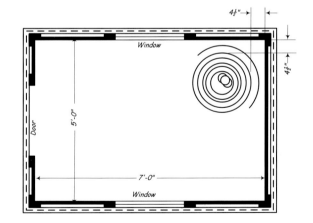

Window

Door

5'-0"

7'-0"

Window

4½"

4½"

ORIGINAL ENGINEER ON FILE
PENNA RAILROAD
OFFICE OF
M.W.

51213
P.R.R. STANDARD
WATCH BOX

APRIL 1, 1879, REVISED JUNE 1911

Redrawn from original PRR drawings by Jeff Scherb

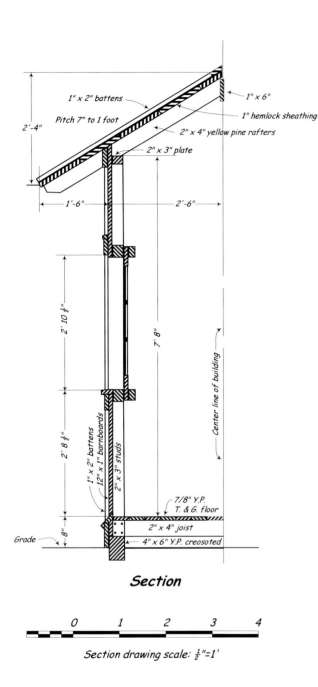

1" x 2" battens

Pitch 7" to 1 foot

1" x 6"

1" hemlock sheathing

2" x 4" yellow pine rafters

2" x 3" plate

2'-4"

1'-6"

2'-6"

2' 10 1/2"

7' 8"

Center line of building

1" x 2" battens

12" x 1" barnboards

2" x 3" studs

2' 8 1/2"

7/8" Y.P. T. & G. floor

2" x 4" joist

Grade

8"

4" x 6" Y.P. creosoted

Section

0   1   2   3   4

Section drawing scale: 1/2" = 1'

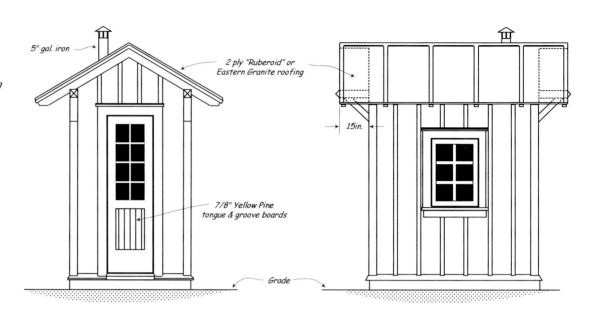

5" gal. iron

2 ply "Ruberoid" or Eastern Granite roofing

7/8" Yellow Pine tongue & groove boards

Grade

15in.

Front Elevation

Side Elevation

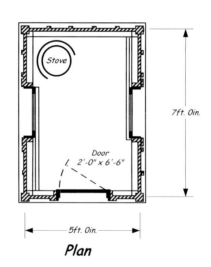

Stove

Door
2'-0" x 6'-6"

7ft. 0in.

5ft. 0in.

Plan

Notes:

A window may be placed in the rear of box when necessary.

All trims, outlookers, facia boards and other outside finish, also the stiles and rails of the doors, are to be painted dark P.R.R. Standard. All panels of doors and other outside woodwork to be painted light P.R.R. Standard.

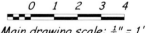

0   1   2   3   4

Main drawing scale: 1/4" = 1'

59329
P.R.R. STANDARD
WATCH BOX
DECEMBER 1911, REVISED APRIL 1914

Redrawn from original P.R.R. drawings by Jeff Scherb

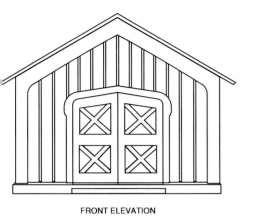

FRONT ELEVATION

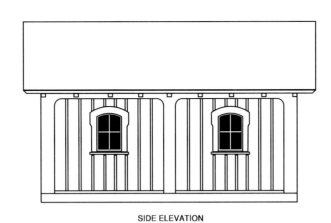

SIDE ELEVATION

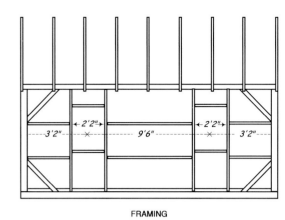

FRAMING

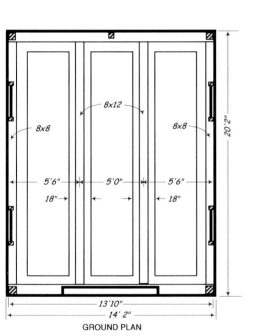

GROUND PLAN

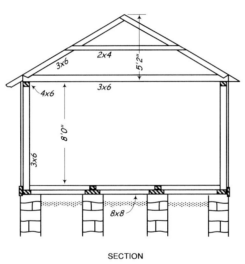

SECTION

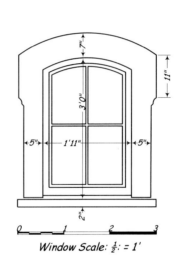

Window Scale: ½: = 1'

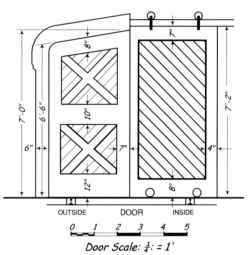

OUTSIDE   DOOR   INSIDE

Door Scale: ¼: = 1'

GENERAL DESIGN TO BE FOLLOWED.   THREE SIZES MAY BE USED.
SIZE "A" 16'-2" WIDE BY 30'-2" LONG. 3 WINDOWS ON EACH SIDE, 7 FT. DOOR.
SIZE "B" 16'-2" WIDE BY 20'-2" LONG   AS PER DRAWING.
SIZE "C" 13'-4" WIDE BY 16'-4" LONG. 2 WINDOWS ON ONE SIDE, 6 FT. DOOR.
FLOOR 2" PLANK ON 3" X 12" JOISTS, SPACED 18" BETWEEN CENTRES,
POST FOUNDATIONS FOR SIZE "C".

0 1 2 3 4 5 6 7 8
Main Drawing Scale:
1:87 (HO scale)

57984
P.R.R. STANDARD
TOOL HOUSE
MARCH 1905
REDRAWN FROM ORIGINAL P.R.R. DRAWINGS BY JEFF SCHERB

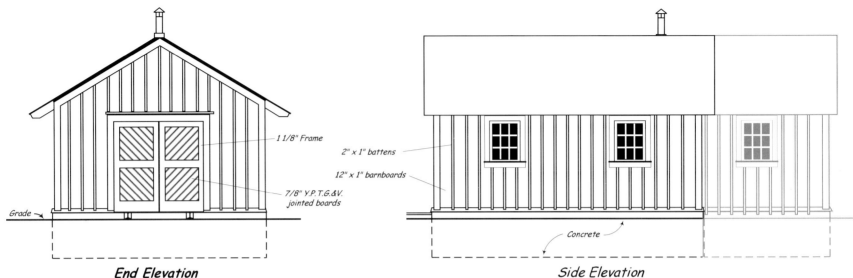

End Elevation

1 1/8" Frame

7/8" Y.P. T.G.&V. jointed boards

Grade

Side Elevation

2" x 1" battens

12" x 1" barnboards

Concrete

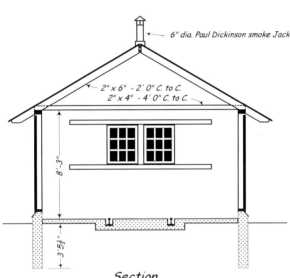

6" dia. Paul Dickinson smoke Jack

2" x 6" - 2' 0" C. to C.
2" x 4" - 4' 0" C. to C.

8' - 3"

3' 5 1/2"

Section

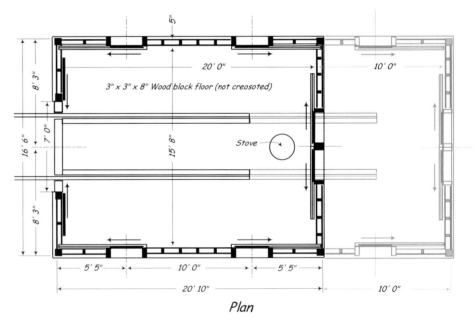

5"

8' 3"

20' 0"

10' 0"

3" x 3" x 8" Wood block floor (not creosoted)

16' 6"

7' 0"

15' 8"

Stove

8' 3"

5' 5"

10' 0"

5' 5"

20' 10"

10' 0"

Plan

Notes:
- Concrete for foundation and floor to be 1:3:6 mixture.
- All exposed exterior lumber to be Cypress or Yellow Pine surfaced.
  All other lumber to be Hemlock or Spruce rough.
- All exterior woodwork to have 3 coats of white lead and linseed oil,
  finish to P.R.R. Standard tints.
- Windows to have G.I. wire screens diamond mesh.
- Gray lines show method of enlarging house.

0 1 2 3 4 5 6 7 8

Scale: 1:87 (HO scale)

59327
P.R.R. STANDARD
TOOL HOUSE
DESIGN "B", OCTOBER 1911

Redrawn from original P.R.R. drawings by Jeff Scherb

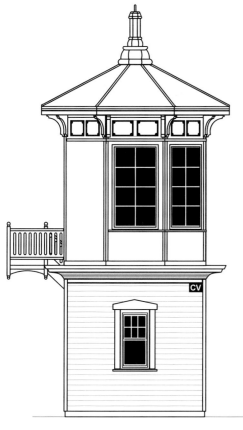

Side Elevation

Track Elevation

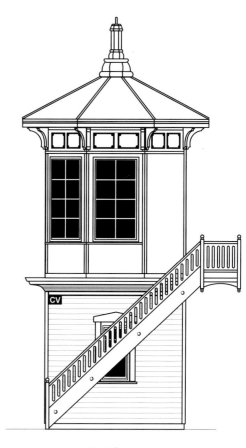

Side Elevation

0 1 2 3 4 5 6 7 8

Scale: 1:87 (HO scale)

PENNSYLVANIA SYSTEM

OCTAGONAL
SIGNAL CABIN
CIRCA 1895
Plate 1 of 2
Drawn by Jeff Scherb

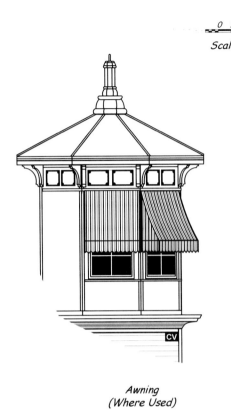

0 1 2 3 4 5 6 7 8

Scale: 1:87 (HO scale)

Awning
(Where Used)

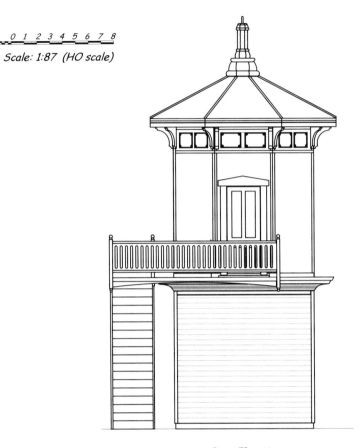

Rear Elevation

Signal Platform
(Where Used)

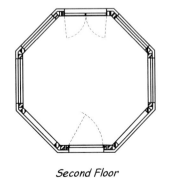

Second Floor

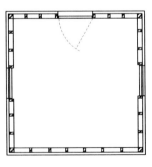

First Floor

PENNSYLVANIA SYSTEM

OCTAGONAL
SIGNAL CABIN
CIRCA 1895
Plate 2 of 2
Drawn by Jeff Scherb

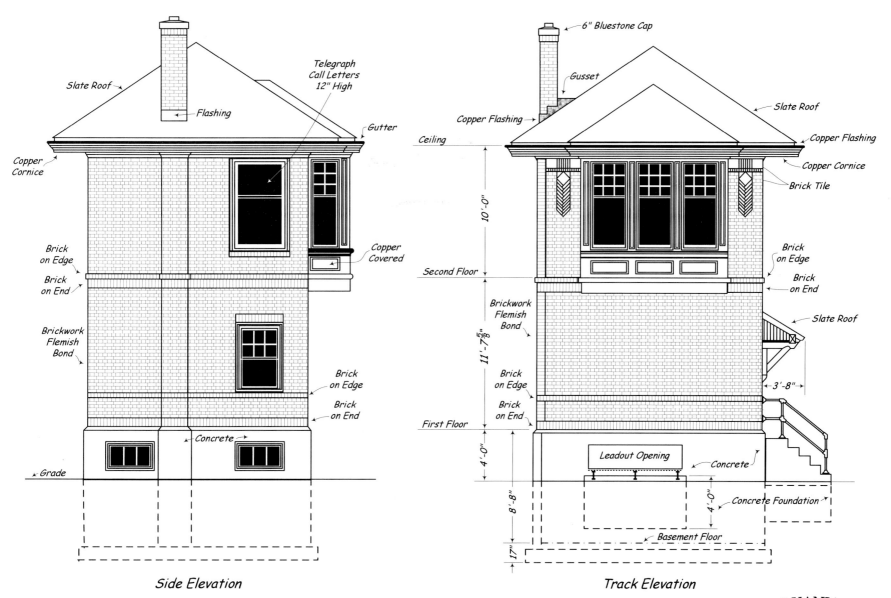

Side Elevation

Track Elevation

SIGNAL CABIN
8 TO 20 LEVER MACHINE
Plate 1 of 3
Drawn by Jeff Scherb

Scale: 1:87 (HO scale)

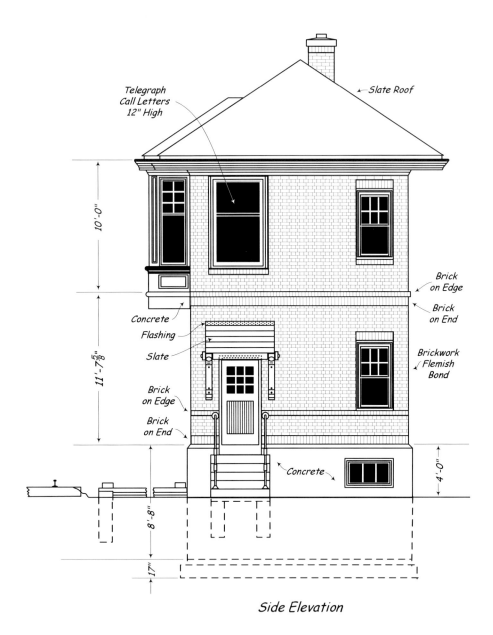

Telegraph
Call Letters
12" High

Slate Roof

10'-0"

Concrete

Flashing

Slate

Brick
on Edge

Brick
on End

Concrete

11'-7⅝"

4'-0"

8'-8"

17"

Brick
on Edge

Brick
on End

Brickwork
Flemish
Bond

Side Elevation

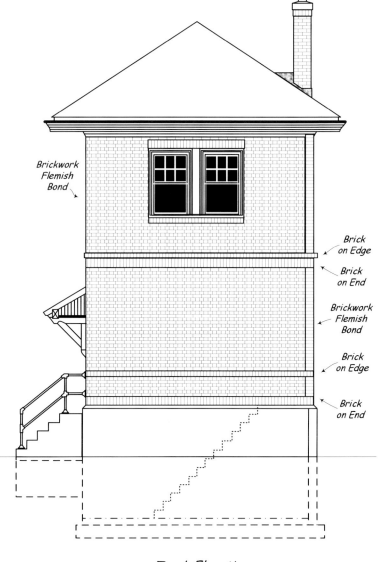

Brickwork
Flemish
Bond

Brick
on Edge

Brick
on End

Brickwork
Flemish
Bond

Brick
on Edge

Brick
on End

Track Elevation

0 1 2 3 4 5 6 7 8

Scale: 1:87 (HO scale)

PENNSYLVANIA SYSTEM

SIGNAL CABIN
8 TO 20 LEVER MACHINE
Plate 2 of 3

Drawn by Jeff Scherb

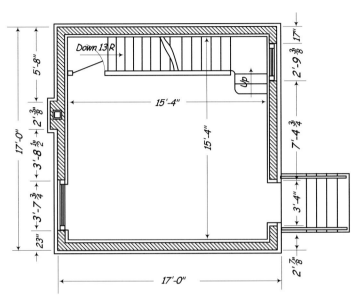

First Floor Plan

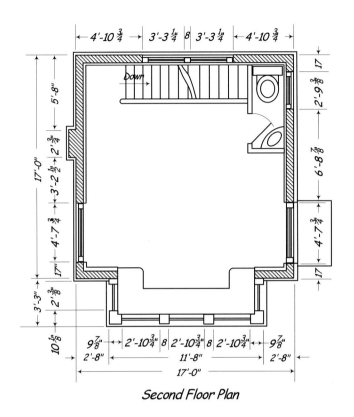

Second Floor Plan

0 1 2 3 4 5 6 7 8

Scale: 1:87 (HO scale)

PENNSYLVANIA SYSTEM

SIGNAL CABIN
8 TO 20 LEVER MACHINE
Plate 3 of 3
Drawn by Jeff Scherb

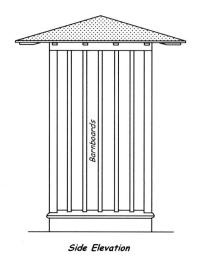

Side Elevation

Barnboards

Front Elevation

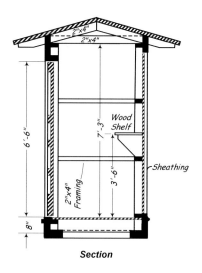

Section

2"x4"
2"x4"
6'-6"
7'-3"
Wood Shelf
Sheathing
2"x4" Framing
3'-6"
8"

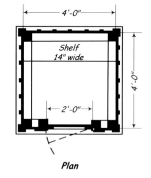

4'-0"

Shelf 14" wide

2'-0"

4'-0"

Plan

0 1 2 3 4

Drawing scale: $\frac{1}{4}$" = 1'

NOTES:

All trims, outlookers, facia boards and other outside finish, also the stiles and rails of the doors, are to be painted dark P.R.R. Standard. All panels of doors and other outside woodwork to be painted light P.R.R. Standard.

Standard switch lock with keys for door.

59443
P.R.R. STANDARD
TELEPHONE BOOTH
(Size 4-0 x 4-0)
JANUARY 1909

Redrawn from original P.R.R. drawings by Jeff Scherb

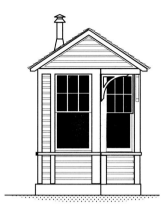

End Elevation

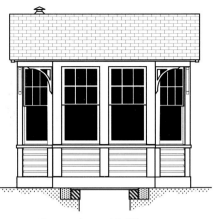

Front (Track) Elevation

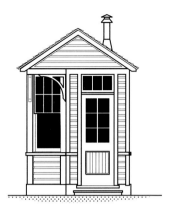

Door End Elevation

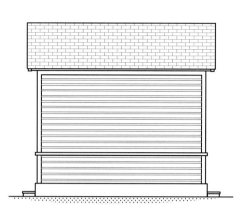

Back Elevation

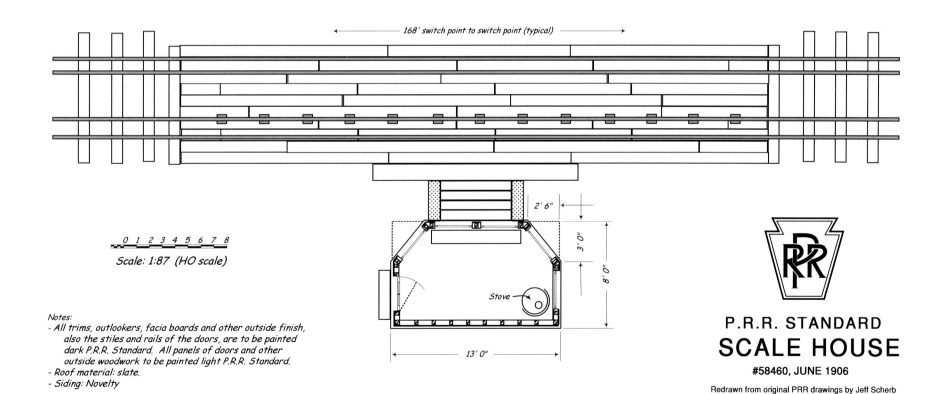

168' switch point to switch point (typical)

0 1 2 3 4 5 6 7 8

Scale: 1:87 (HO scale)

2' 6"

3' 0"

8' 0"

Stove

13' 0"

Notes:
- All trims, outlookers, facia boards and other outside finish,
  also the stiles and rails of the doors, are to be painted
  dark P.R.R. Standard. All panels of doors and other
  outside woodwork to be painted light P.R.R. Standard.
- Roof material: slate.
- Siding: Novelty

P.R.R. STANDARD

SCALE HOUSE

#58460, JUNE 1906

Redrawn from original PRR drawings by Jeff Scherb

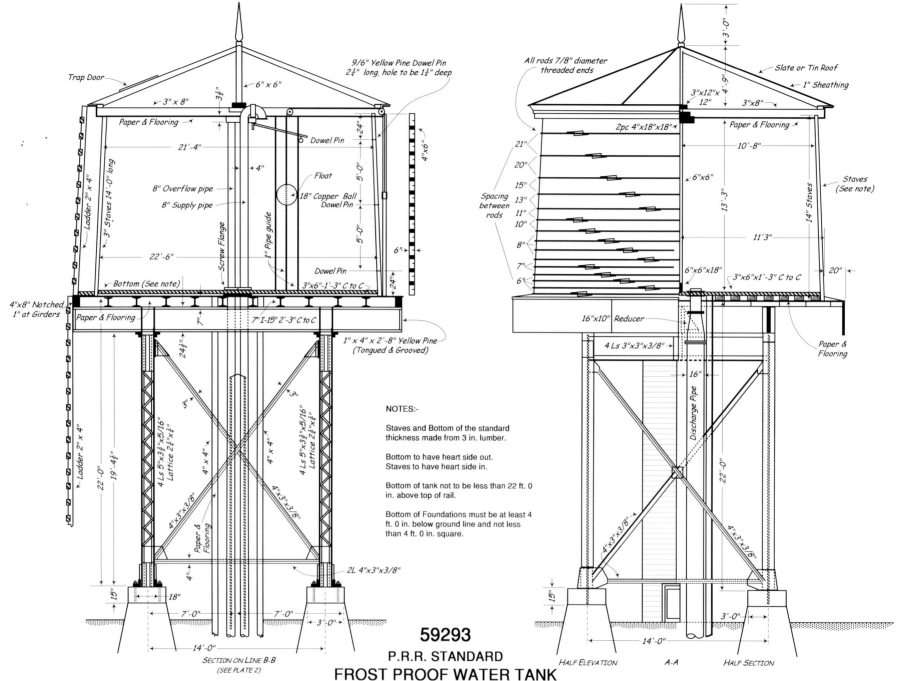

59293

P.R.R. STANDARD

FROST PROOF WATER TANK

CAPACITY 35,000 GALLONS

PLATE 1 of 2

SEPTEMBER 1904, REVISED OCTOBER 1912
REDRAWN FROM ORIGINAL P.R.R. DRAWINGS BY JEFF SCHERB

NOTES:-

Staves and Bottom of the standard thickness made from 3 in. lumber.

Bottom to have heart side out. Staves to have heart side in.

Bottom of tank not to be less than 22 ft. 0 in. above top of rail.

Bottom of Foundations must be at least 4 ft. 0 in. below ground line and not less than 4 ft. 0 in. square.

Scale: 1:87 (HO scale)

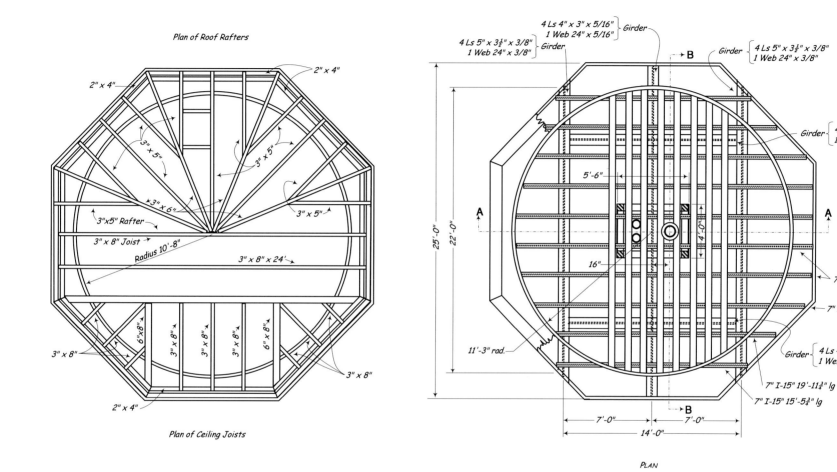

Plan of Roof Rafters

2" x 4"
3" x 5"
3" x 5"
3" x 5"
3" x 6"
3" x 5"
3"x5" Rafter
3" x 8" Joist
Radius 10'-8"
3" x 8" x 24'
2" x 4"
6" x 8"
3" x 8"
3" x 8"
3" x 8"
6" x 8"
3" x 8"
3" x 8"
2" x 4"
3" x 8"

Plan of Ceiling Joists

4 Ls 4" x 3" x 5/16"
1 Web 24" x 5/16"   Girder
4 Ls 5" x 3½" x 3/8"
1 Web 24" x 3/8"   Girder
B
Girder   4 Ls 5" x 3½" x 3/8"
1 Web 24" x 3/8"
Girder   4 Ls 4" x 3" x 5/16"
1 Web 24" x 5/16"
5'-6"
25'-0"
22'-0"
A   A
4'-0"
7" I-15" 25'-6 lg
16"
7" I-15" 24'-5¾" lg
11'-3" rad.
Girder   4 Ls 4" x 3" x 5/16"
1 Web 24" x 5/16"
7" I-15" 19'-11¾" lg
7" I-15" 15'-5¾" lg
B
7'-0"   7'-0"
14'-0"

PLAN

59293
P.R.R. STANDARD
FROST PROOF WATER TANK
CAPACITY 35,000 GALLONS
PLATE 2 of 2
SEPTEMBER 1904, REVISED OCTOBER 1912
REDRAWN FROM ORIGINAL P.R.R. DRAWINGS BY JEFF SCHERB

0 1 2 3 4 5 6 7 8
Scale: 1:87 (HO scale)

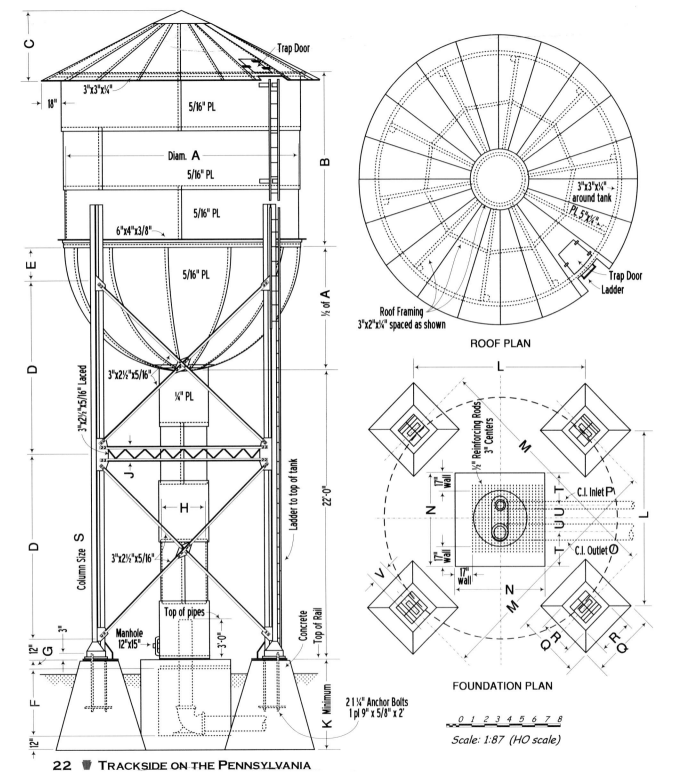

Trap Door

3"x3"x¼"

18"

5/16" PL

5/16" PL

Diam. A

5/16" PL

5/16" PL

6"x4"x3/8"

5/16" PL

3"x2½"x5/16" Laced

3"x2½"x5/16"

¼" PL

3"x2½"x5/16"

J

H

Top of pipes

Column Size S

Ladder to top of tank

B

½ of A

22'-0"

D

D

E

C

G
12"

3"

3'-0"

F

12"

K Minimum

Concrete

Top of Rail

Manhole 12"x15"

2 1¼" Anchor Bolts
1 pl 9" x 5/8" x 2'

ROOF PLAN

3"x3"x¼" around tank

PL 5"x¼"

Trap Door Ladder

Roof Framing 3"x2"x¼" spaced as shown

FOUNDATION PLAN

L

M

N

½" Reinforcing Rods 3" Centers

17" wall

17" wall

17" wall

N

T U U T

C.I. Inlet P

C.I. Outlet O

L

M

V

Q R R Q

0 1 2 3 4 5 6 7 8

Scale: 1:87 (HO scale)

CAPACITY OF TANKS

Dimension	35,000 Gallons	50,000 Gallons	75,000 Gallons	100,000 Gallons
A	18'-0"	20'-0"	24'-0"	26'-0"
B	13'-0"	15'-0"	14'-0"	17'-0"
C	5'-3"	5'-9"	6'-9"	7'-3"
D	13'-9"	14'-0"	14'-6"	14'-6"
E	2'-6"	3'-0"	4'-0"	5'-0"
F	4'-2"	4'-2"	5'-2"	6'-0"
G	10"	10"	10"	12"
H	4'-0"	4'-0"	4'-0"	5'-0"
J	10"	10"	10"	12"
K	6'-0"	6'-0"	7'-0"	8'-0"
L	13'-3"	14'-9 1/2"	17'-7 1/2"	19'-1 3/4"
M	18'-8 7/8"	20'-10 3/8"	24'-11 1/8"	27'-0 7/8"
N	7'-0"	7'-0"	7'-0"	8'-0"
O	14"	14"	18"	20"
P	6"	8"	8"	18"
Q	5'-0"	6'-0"	7'-6"	9'-6"
R	2'-4"	2'-4"	2'-6"	2'-6"
S	4L 4"x3"x3/8"	4L 4"x3"x7/16"	4L 5"x3 1/2"x9/16"	4L 6"x4"x9/16"
T	2'-6"	2'-6"	2'-6"	2'-9"
U	1'-0"	1'-0"	1'-0"	1'-3"
V	14"	16"	16 1/2"	18"

NOTE:-

Rivets in roof plates to be 3/8" diam. - 4 " pitch. Rivets in tank plates to be 5/8" diam. - 2" pitch. Rivets in other members 3/4" diam. including the connection of the tank to the columns All seams of tank to be single rivetted, lap joints except vertical seams of 1st ring in shell which are double rivetted, lap joints.

Foundations and pipe furnished by P.R.R. Co. Foundation bolts to be furnished in advance by Tank Contractor. Tank and support to be furnished and erected by the Tank Contractor.

Painting to be done by P.R.R. Co. as follows:- After erection Steel Work shall be thoroughly cleaned from rust and painted with three coats of paint. 1st two coats to be 20lbs. red lead 1lb. lamp black and 1 pint Japan dryer to 1 gallon raw linseed oil. 3rd coat to be P.R.R. Specification Standard Black.

61970

STANDARD
STEEL WATER TANKS
35,000, 50,000, 75,000 & 100,000 Gallons Capacity
PHILA., FEBRUARY 1916
REDRAWN FROM ORIGINAL PRR DRAWINGS BY JEFF SCHERB

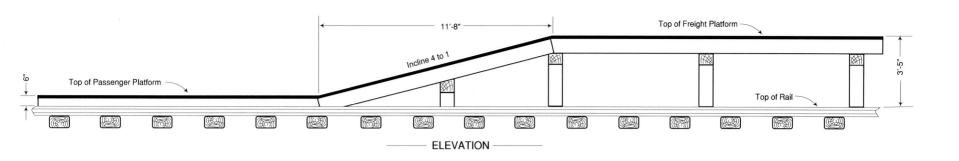

ELEVATION

Top of Freight Platform

11'-8"

Incline 4 to 1

Top of Passenger Platform

6"

3'-5"

Top of Rail

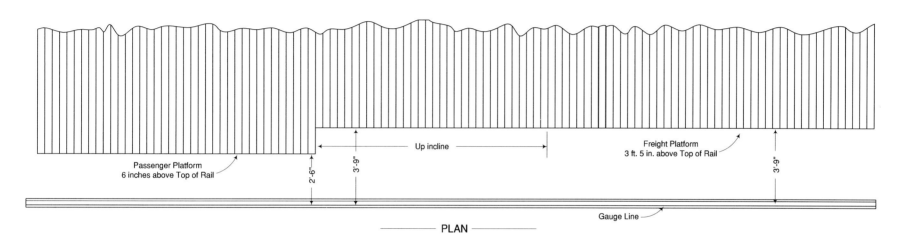

PLAN

Passenger Platform
6 inches above Top of Rail

Up incline

Freight Platform
3 ft. 5 in. above Top of Rail

2'-6"

3'-9"

3'-9"

Gauge Line

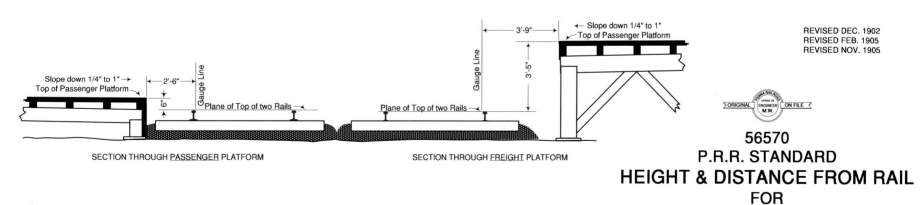

Slope down 1/4" to 1"
Top of Passenger Platform

2'-6"

Gauge Line

6"

Plane of Top of two Rails

SECTION THROUGH <u>PASSENGER</u> PLATFORM

Plane of Top of two Rails

Gauge Line

3'-9"

Slope down 1/4" to 1"
Top of Passenger Platform

3'-5"

SECTION THROUGH <u>FREIGHT</u> PLATFORM

REVISED DEC. 1902
REVISED FEB. 1905
REVISED NOV. 1905

ORIGINAL — PENNA RAIL ROAD OFFICE OF ENGINEER M.W. — ON FILE

56570
P.R.R. STANDARD
HEIGHT & DISTANCE FROM RAIL
FOR
PASSENGER AND FREIGHT PLATFORMS
JUNE, 1902
Redrawn from original P.R.R. drawings by Jeff Scherb

0"   1"   2"   3"   4"   6"

SCALE

BRIDGES AND CULVERTS

Bridges and Culverts

THE TERRITORY COVERED by the Pennsylvania, while not generally mountainous, nevertheless required a great many bridges and culverts. These ranged from small culverts over Appalachian mountain streams to engineering monuments such as the Hell Gate Bridge, with a center span of 977.5 feet; it was the largest arch in the world at the time of its construction. The total length of the structure, from the abutment on Long Island to the abutment in the Bronx, was over three miles.

In the earliest years, arches of cut stone construction were used. Many examples of these bridges, some built as early as the 1850s, are still in good repair and being used daily in this century. The 3,830-foot long Rockville Bridge, built from 1900-1902 across the Susquehanna River near Harrisburg, is the longest stone masonry arch bridge in the world, and is still in use today, 100 years later. This bridge consists of 48 arch spans, each 40′ in length.

For larger applications, steel truss bridges were often used, these being supplied by one of the many bridge companies of the day, and being designed, or at least configured, specifically for the site out of standard catalog designs. At the intersection of navigable rivers and the railroad, movable bridges were often used, also from leading bridge designers of the day, such as vertical lift bridges of Waddell & Harrington design, or rolling lift bridges by the Scherzer Rolling Lift Bridge Company of Chicago. One notable example still in use today is the three-track vertical lift bridge over the Passaic River at Newark's Pennsylvania Station. This bridge was the largest of its type in the world at the time of its construction, and may still be.

The most numerous type of railroad "bridge" is the culvert, a small opening through the roadbed for drainage or passage of small streams. These are installed wherever water must cross the right-of-way, and are especially common in the hilly Pennsylvania Railroad territory. Many of the smallest culverts were nothing more than corrugated pipes laid through the roadbed, but for more drainage or larger streams, the Pennsylvania specified concrete arch culverts (p. 28), which are the strongest type. Not often modeled, a roadbed perforated by culverts can add a great deal of realism to the model right-of-way.

Early in its history, the Pennsylvania built many stone arches, and while perhaps not as prolific a user of the type as other Northeastern railroads, the Pennsylvania did employ concrete arch bridges as well (p. 29). Stone was generally used until about 1900, when either concrete arches, or steel-arch or truss bridges became more common. A number of magnificent multiple spandrel concrete arch bridges are still in use today in northeastern Pennsylvania, and while the Lackawanna Railroad is best known for the type, the epitome of which was the Nicholson Bridge (also known as the Tunkhannock Viaduct), the Pennsylvania also employed these in the Northeast, a prime example being the Manayunk Bridge.

Large multi-arch viaducts such as these were custom-designed for each site, but smaller spans were built to a standard design. The standard design for spans of 10 to 80 feet specified a simple semicircular arch. Longer bridges would be made of multiple simple arches.

The move to concrete arches and away from stone arch construction was made around 1900, when poured concrete technology matured to the point that large structures became practical. Concrete arches were quicker and cheaper to construct than stone arches, and it was easier to form more complex arch shapes, such as skewed spans or non-circular arches. It is interesting to note, though, that through southeastern Pennsylvania at least, many of the stone arches built in the middle of the 19th century are in better condition today than the concrete arches built 50 or 75 years later.

As a side note, a bridge consisting of a single arch is known as an arch bridge, and a bridge consisting of multiple arches is generally known as a viaduct.

As the railroad expanded, more efficient and economical means of construction were needed, so timber trestles came into common use. Expedient to construct, these trestles were often replaced by more permanent structures later, or in some cases, a trestle might become a fill by dumping fill dirt over the sides until the earth had been built up to the level of the tracks.

The Pennsylvania had two common standard designs for trestles. One of these designs was of the *pile* type (p. 32), and the other was the *framed* type (p. 33). The vertical members, or bents, of a pile trestle are made from round lumber, typically driven into the ground with a pile driver. A framed trestle uses square lumber, and rather than being driven into the ground, the bents rest on sills, which in turn rest on concrete or stone foundations. The bents of pile trestles generally extend from the ground to the track, while framed trestle bents may consist of multiple stories of timbers, with each story resting on a sill, which rests on the bents of the lower story. Framed trestles of this construction can be much higher than pile trestles, since the height of the pile trestle is limited to the maximum length of the single piece of lumber forming the pile. Framed trestles also don't require the use of a pile driver, since the timbers rest on a stone or concrete foundation. Pile construction is often used for low trestles over marshy ground that would require sinking foundations deep enough to reach solid ground, and framed construction is used for heights exceeding the maximum length of available piles, or for locations where footings can be placed on solid ground.

Trestles are also used for the delivery of bulk commodities, such as coal. Coal trestles (pp. 36 and 37) started appearing in the 1880s, as a more efficient way of unloading coal from hoppers for use in fueling steam locomotives. Hoppers were pushed up onto a trestle, and coal was unloaded by opening the hopper doors and letting it fall through the tracks to storage bins below. By the 1940s, coal trestles had become fairly rare, with most being replaced by coaling stations with mechanical lifts.

The other use for coal trestles was in commercial coal yards, and these were still quite common into the Fifties. Hoppers would deliver the coal from these trestles into bins where is was then loaded into trucks for delivery to homes or businesses, or sold at the coal yard by the pound. Coal was the most common fuel for heating homes and businesses until after World War II, when conversion to oil took place, and every town had at least one retail coal dealer. In 1925, there were about 40,000 retail coal dealers in the United States, which works out to about one for every 650 homes. As home heating moved away from coal and toward oil or gas, many of these coal yards went out of business, but quite a few adapted to the new technology and began selling heating oil. Built on a hill, these common small coal yards make ideal businesses for a model railroad. They provide for great operating interest, don't take up a great deal of space, and provide a great destination for hoppers from a mine operation. A coal yard adapting to the times and dealing in heating oil also makes a good destination for tank cars. ♥

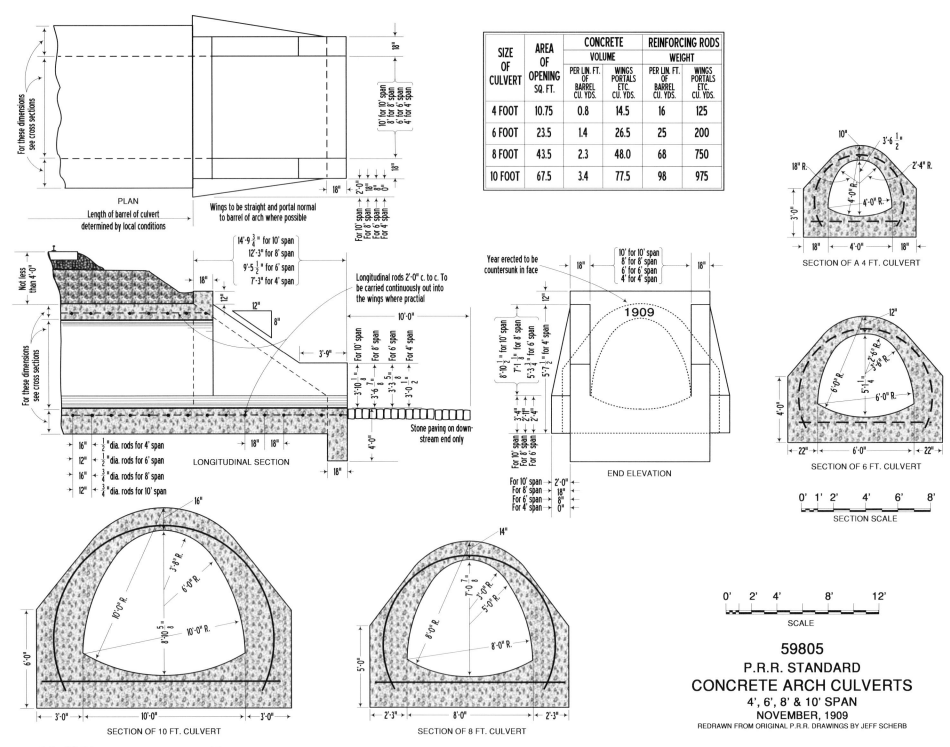

SIZE OF CULVERT	AREA OF OPENING SQ. FT.	CONCRETE		REINFORCING RODS	
		VOLUME		WEIGHT	
		PER LIN. FT. OF BARREL CU. YDS.	WINGS PORTALS ETC. CU. YDS.	PER LIN. FT. OF BARREL CU. YDS.	WINGS PORTALS ETC. CU. YDS.
4 FOOT	10.75	0.8	14.5	16	125
6 FOOT	23.5	1.4	26.5	25	200
8 FOOT	43.5	2.3	48.0	68	750
10 FOOT	67.5	3.4	77.5	98	975

PLAN

Length of barrel of culvert determined by local conditions

Wings to be straight and portal normal to barrel of arch where possible

LONGITUDINAL SECTION

Year erected to be countersunk in face

1909

END ELEVATION

SECTION OF A 4 FT. CULVERT

SECTION OF 6 FT. CULVERT

SECTION SCALE

SECTION OF 10 FT. CULVERT

SECTION OF 8 FT. CULVERT

SCALE

59805
P.R.R. STANDARD
CONCRETE ARCH CULVERTS
4', 6', 8' & 10' SPAN
NOVEMBER, 1909
REDRAWN FROM ORIGINAL P.R.R. DRAWINGS BY JEFF SCHERB

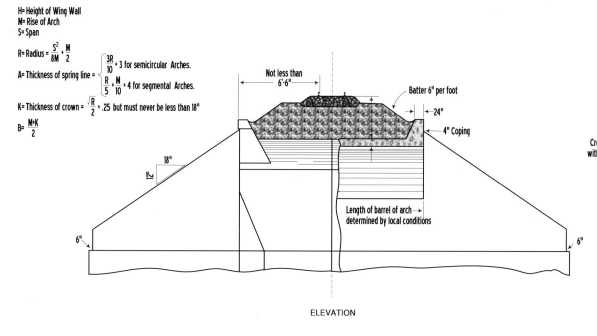

H= Height of Wing Wall
M= Rise of Arch
S= Span

$R = \text{Radius} = \dfrac{S^2}{8M} + \dfrac{M}{2}$

$A = \text{Thickness of spring line} = \begin{cases} \dfrac{3R}{10} + 3 \text{ for semicircular Arches.} \\[2mm] \dfrac{R}{5} + \dfrac{M}{10} + 4 \text{ for segmental Arches.} \end{cases}$

$K = \text{Thickness of crown} = \dfrac{\sqrt{R}}{2} + .25$ but must never be less than 18"

$B = \dfrac{M+K}{2}$

Not less than 6'-6"

Batter 6" per foot

24"

4" Coping

18"

12"

Length of barrel of arch → determined by local conditions

6"   6"

ELEVATION

NOTE:-
All wings should be straight unless local conditions make it absolutely necessary to construct them otherwise.
Backs of Abutments, Wings and Parapets may be stepped, when desired, providing cross-section of Masonry is not decreased.
Proportions of cement, sand and stone to be in accordance with P.R.R. Specifications.

18"

Crown of arch to be thoroughly covered with an approved water proofing material

1912

K

M.

Not less than $\dfrac{S}{5}$

R.

S.

H.

B.

18"

Batter in inches per ft. of height = $\dfrac{S \text{ (in feet)}}{2M \text{ (in feet)}}$

6"   6"

6"

6"

4H

Batter $\frac{1}{2}$" per ft.

Foundation down to firm material

Not more than 2A otherwise determined by local conditions

SECTION A-A

P = Thickness of Pier =

4'-0" For Spans of 10'-0" to 20'-0"
5'-0"   "   " of 20'-0" to 35'-0"
6'-0"   "   " of 35'-0" to 50'-0"
7'-0"   "   " of 50'-0" to 70'-0"
8'-0"   "   " of 70'-0" to 80'-0"

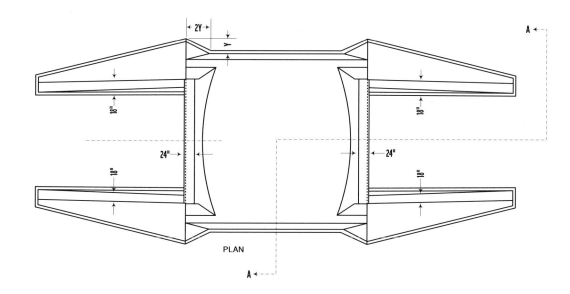

A ←

2Y

Y

18"

18"

24"   24"

18"   18"

PLAN

A ←

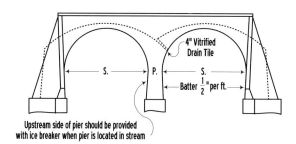

4" Vitrified Drain Tile

S.   P.   S.

Batter $\frac{1}{2}$" per ft.

Upstream side of pier should be provided with ice breaker when pier is located in stream

59293
P.R.R. STANDARD
CONCRETE ARCH BRIDGE
OF SPANS BETWEEN
10 FEET AND 80 FEET
AUGUST 1912
REDRAWN FROM ORIGINAL P.R.R. DRAWINGS BY JEFF SCHERB

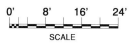

0'   8'   16'   24'

SCALE

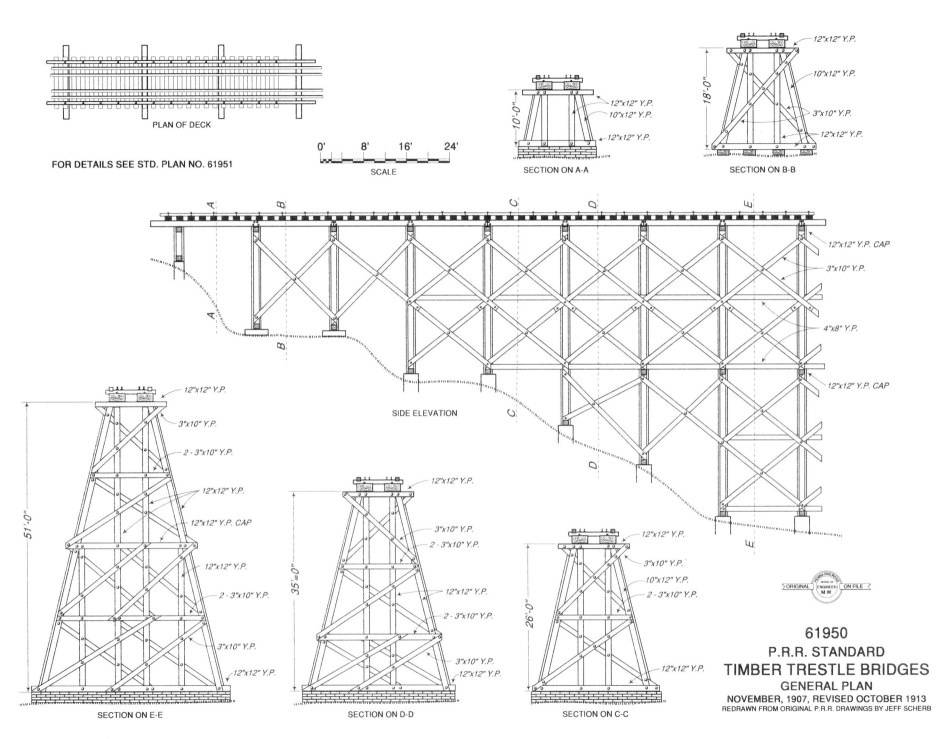

PLAN OF DECK

FOR DETAILS SEE STD. PLAN NO. 61951

SCALE

0'   8'   16'   24'

SECTION ON A-A

12"x12" Y.P.
10"x12" Y.P.
12"x12" Y.P.

10'-0"

SECTION ON B-B

12"x12" Y.P.
10"x12" Y.P.
3"x10" Y.P.
12"x12" Y.P.

18'-0"

SIDE ELEVATION

12"x12" Y.P. CAP
3"x10" Y.P.
4"x8" Y.P.
12"x12" Y.P. CAP

SECTION ON E-E

51'-0"

12"x12" Y.P.
3"x10" Y.P.
2 - 3"x10" Y.P.
12"x12" Y.P.
12"x12" Y.P. CAP
12"x12" Y.P.
2 - 3"x10" Y.P.
3"x10" Y.P.
12"x12" Y.P.

SECTION ON D-D

35'-0"

12"x12" Y.P.
3"x10" Y.P.
2 - 3"x10" Y.P.
12"x12" Y.P.
2 - 3"x10" Y.P.
3"x10" Y.P.
12"x12" Y.P.

SECTION ON C-C

26'-0"

12"x12" Y.P.
3"x10" Y.P.
10"x12" Y.P.
2 - 3"x10" Y.P.
12"x12" Y.P.

61950
P.R.R. STANDARD
TIMBER TRESTLE BRIDGES
GENERAL PLAN
NOVEMBER, 1907, REVISED OCTOBER 1913
REDRAWN FROM ORIGINAL P.R.R. DRAWINGS BY JEFF SCHERB

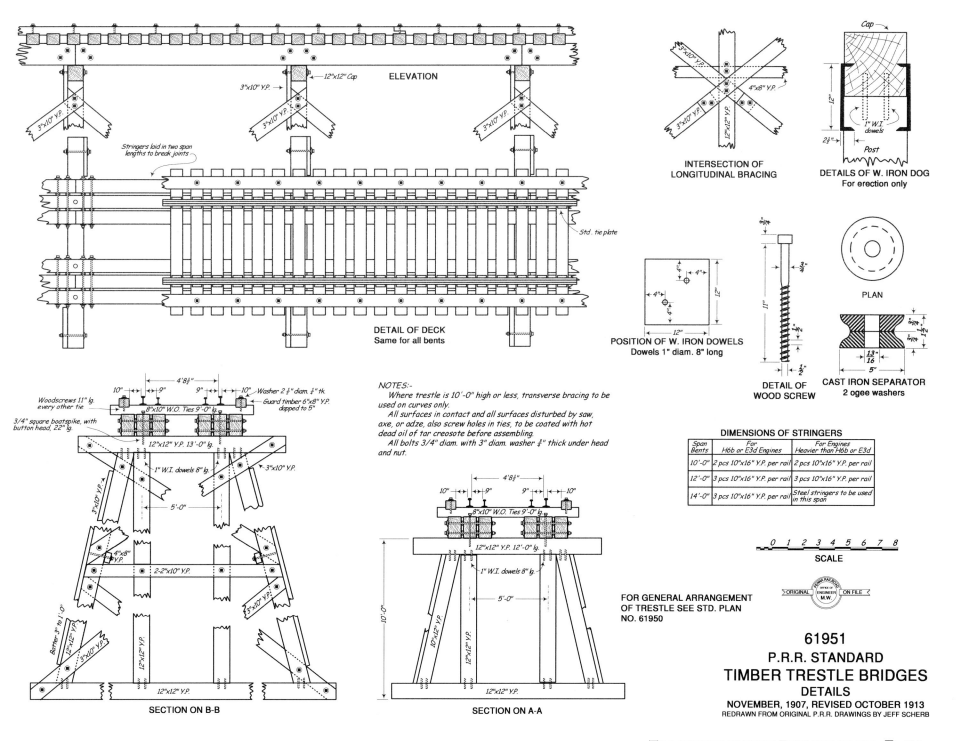

ELEVATION

12"x12" Cap

3"x10" Y.P.

3"x10" Y.P.

3"x10" Y.P.

3"x10" Y.P.

Stringers laid in two span
lengths to break joints

Std. tie plate

DETAIL OF DECK
Same for all bents

INTERSECTION OF
LONGITUDINAL BRACING

3"x10" Y.P.

4"x8" Y.P.

3"x10" Y.P.

12"x12" Y.P.

Cap

DETAILS OF W. IRON DOG
For erection only

1" W.I. dowels

Post

POSITION OF W. IRON DOWELS
Dowels 1" diam. 8" long

DETAIL OF
WOOD SCREW

PLAN

CAST IRON SEPARATOR
2 ogee washers

4'8½"

10"   9"   9"   10"

Washer 2½" diam. ¼" tk.
Guard timber 6"x8" Y.P.
dapped to 5"

Woodscrews 11" lg.
every other tie

8"x10" W.O. Ties 9'-0" lg.

3/4" square boatspike, with
button head, 22" lg.

12"x12" Y.P. 13'-0" lg.

1" W.I. dowels 8" lg.

3"x10" Y.P.

3"x10" Y.P.

5'-0"

4"x8"
Y.P.

2-2"x10" Y.P.

3"x10" Y.P.

Batter 3" to 1'-0"

12"x12" Y.P.

3"x10" Y.P.

12"x12" Y.P.

SECTION ON B-B

NOTES:-
   Where trestle is 10'-0" high or less, transverse bracing to be
used on curves only.
   All surfaces in contact and all surfaces disturbed by saw,
axe, or adze, also screw holes in ties, to be coated with hot
dead oil of tar creosote before assembling.
   All bolts 3/4" diam. with 3" diam. washer ⅜" thick under head
and nut.

4'8½"

10"   9"   9"   10"

8"x10" W.O. Ties 9'-0" lg.

12"x12" Y.P. 12'-0" lg.

1" W.I. dowels 8" lg.

5'-0"

10'-0"

10"x12" Y.P.

12"x12" Y.P.

12"x12" Y.P.

SECTION ON A-A

FOR GENERAL ARRANGEMENT
OF TRESTLE SEE STD. PLAN
NO. 61950

DIMENSIONS OF STRINGERS

Span Bents	For H6b or E3d Engines	For Engines Heavier than H6b or E3d
10'-0"	2 pcs 10"x16" Y.P. per rail	2 pcs 10"x16" Y.P. per rail
12'-0"	3 pcs 10"x16" Y.P. per rail	3 pcs 10"x16" Y.P. per rail
14'-0"	3 pcs 10"x16" Y.P. per rail	Steel stringers to be used in this span

0 1 2 3 4 5 6 7 8
SCALE

ORIGINAL PENNA. RAILROAD OFFICE OF ENGINEER M.W. ON FILE

61951
P.R.R. STANDARD
TIMBER TRESTLE BRIDGES
DETAILS
NOVEMBER, 1907, REVISED OCTOBER 1913
REDRAWN FROM ORIGINAL P.R.R. DRAWINGS BY JEFF SCHERB

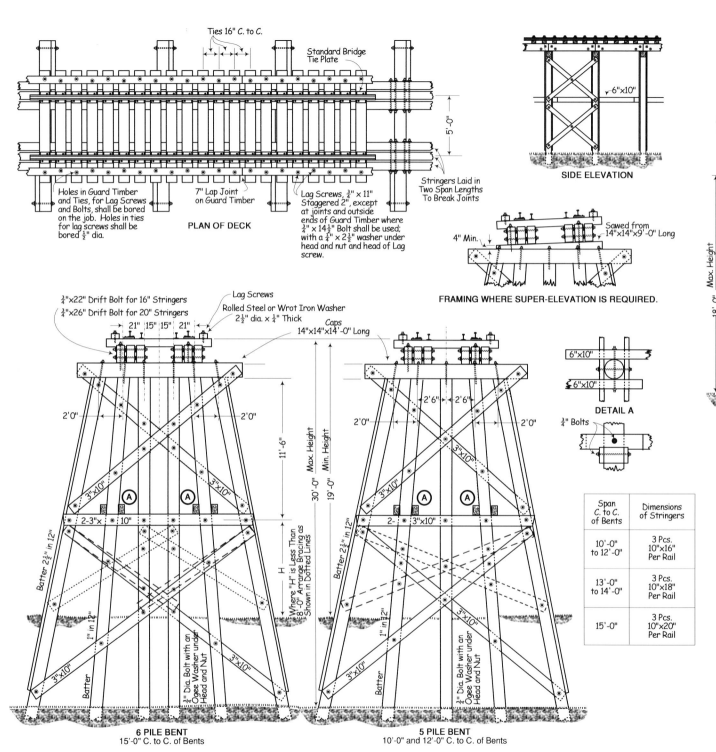
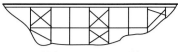
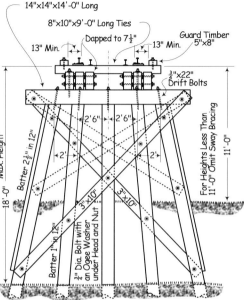

Ties 16" C. to C.

Standard Bridge Tie Plate

5'-0"

Holes in Guard Timber and Ties, for Lag Screws and Bolts, shall be bored on the job. Holes in ties for lag screws shall be bored ½" dia.

7" Lap Joint on Guard Timber

PLAN OF DECK

Lag Screws, ¾" x 11" Staggered 2", except at joints and outside ends of Guard Timber where ¾" x 14½" Bolt shall be used; with a ¼" x 2½" washer under head and nut and head of Lag screw.

Stringers Laid in Two Span Lengths To Break Joints

SIDE ELEVATION

6"×10"

LONGITUDINAL BRACING

Sawed from 14"×14"×9'-0" Long

4" Min.

FRAMING WHERE SUPER-ELEVATION IS REQUIRED.

14"×14"×14'-0" Long

8"×10"×9'-0" Long Ties

Dapped to 7½"

13" Min.   13" Min.

Guard Timber 5"×8"

¾"×22" Drift Bolts

2'6"   2'6"

2'   2'

Max. Height 18'-0"

For Heights Less Than 11'-0" Omit Sway Bracing

11'-0"

Batter 2½" in 12"

¾" Dia. Bolt with an Ogee Washer under Head and Nut

3"×10"   3"×10"

5 PILE BENT
10'-0" and 12'-0" C. to C. of Bents
SAME BRACING SHALL BE USED ON 5 AND 6 PILE BENTS
11'-0" TO 18'-0" HIGH

¾"×22" Drift Bolt for 16" Stringers
¾"×26" Drift Bolt for 20" Stringers

Lag Screws
Rolled Steel or Wrot Iron Washer 2½" dia. x ¼" Thick

Caps 14"×14"×14'-0" Long

21" 15" 15" 21"

2'0"   2'0"

Max. Height 30'-0"   Min. Height 19'-0"

11'-6"

Where "H" is Less Than 8'-0" Arrange Bracing as Shown in Dotted Lines

2-3"x   10"

Batter 2½" in 12"

3"×10"

1" in 12"

Batter

¾" Dia. Bolt with an Ogee Washer under Head and Nut

6 PILE BENT
15'-0" C. to C. of Bents

2'0"   2'0"

2'6"   2'6"

2- 3"×10"

3"×10"

Batter 2½" in 12"

1" in 12"

Batter

¾" Dia. Bolt with an Ogee Washer under Head and Nut

5 PILE BENT
10'-0" and 12'-0" C. to C. of Bents

6"×10"

6"×10"

DETAIL A

¾" Bolts

Span C. to C. of Bents	Dimensions of Stringers
10'-0" to 12'-0"	3 Pcs. 10"x16" Per Rail
13'-0" to 14'-0"	3 Pcs. 10"x18" Per Rail
15'-0"	3 Pcs. 10"x20" Per Rail

Note:-
For all new trestles, and where practicable, use spans 12 feet 0 inches center to center.
Wood may be oak, long leaf yellow pine, of Oregon Fir.
Where Oak is available as to price and delivery it shall have preference for caps and ties.
All wood shall be treated in accordance with the Specifications for the Preservative Treatment of Wood by Pressure Processes.
All cuts, holes, etc., made subsequent to treatment shall be painted in accordance with the Specifications for the Preservative Treatment of Wood by Painting with Creosote Oil.
Lag Screws and Cast Iron Separators (2 Ogee Washers) shall be made as shown on Standard Plan - basic number - 79301.
The maximum permissible speed on Timber Trestles shall be 40 miles per hour.
The maximum super-elevation on Timber Trestles shall be 4 inches.
Speed restriction and super-elevation on Timber Trestles, except as limited above, shall be in accordance with Part 11, Specifications for Standard Track (construction).

THE PENNSYLVANIA RAILROAD
STANDARD
5 AND 6 PILE
TIMBER TRESTLE BRIDGES - OPEN DECK

STANDARD 79300-B, APRIL 1925

Redrawn from original PRR drawings by Jeff Scherb

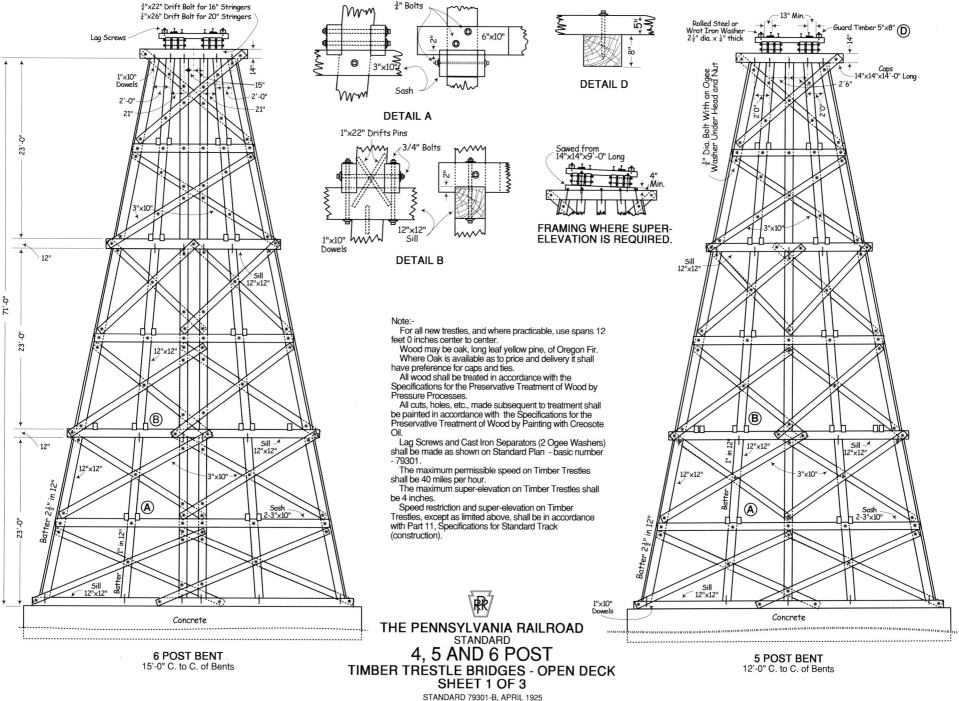

¾"x22" Drift Bolt for 16" Stringers
¾"x26" Drift Bolt for 20" Stringers

Lag Screws

1"x10" Dowels
2'-0"
21"
15"
2'-0"
21"

3"x10"

14"

23'-0"
71'-0"
23'-0"
23'-0"

12"

Sill 12"x12"

12"x12"

Ⓑ

12"x12"

Batter 2½" in 12"

3"x10"

12"

Sill 12"x12"

Ⓐ

Batter 1" in 12"

Sash 2-3"x10"

Batter 1" in 12"

Sill 12"x12"

Batter

Concrete

6 POST BENT
15'-0" C. to C. of Bents

¾" Bolts

2"

6"x10"

3"x10"

Sash

DETAIL A

1"x22" Drifts Pins

3/4" Bolts

2"

1"x10" Dowels

12"x12" Sill

DETAIL B

5"

8"

DETAIL D

Sawed from 14"x14"x9'-0" Long

4" Min.

FRAMING WHERE SUPER-
ELEVATION IS REQUIRED.

Note:-
For all new trestles, and where practicable, use spans 12 feet 0 inches center to center.
Wood may be oak, long leaf yellow pine, of Oregon Fir.
Where Oak is available as to price and delivery it shall have preference for caps and ties.
All wood shall be treated in accordance with the Specifications for the Preservative Treatment of Wood by Pressure Processes.
All cuts, holes, etc., made subsequent to treatment shall be painted in accordance with the Specifications for the Preservative Treatment of Wood by Painting with Creosote Oil.
Lag Screws and Cast Iron Separators (2 Ogee Washers) shall be made as shown on Standard Plan - basic number - 79301.
The maximum permissible speed on Timber Trestles shall be 40 miles per hour.
The maximum super-elevation on Timber Trestles shall be 4 inches.
Speed restriction and super-elevation on Timber Trestles, except as limited above, shall be in accordance with Part 11, Specifications for Standard Track (construction).

Rolled Steel or Wrot Iron Washer 2½" dia. x ¼" thick

13" Min.

Guard Timber 5"x8" Ⓓ

14"

Caps 14"x14"x14'-0" Long

2'-6"

2'0"

2'0"

¾" Dia. Bolt With an Ogee Washer Under Head and Nut

3"x10"

Sill 12"x12"

Ⓑ

12"x12"

Batter 1" in 12"

Sill 12"x12"

3"x10"

Ⓐ

Sash 2-3"x10"

Batter 2½" in 12"

Sill 12"x12"

1"x10" Dowels

Concrete

5 POST BENT
12'-0" C. to C. of Bents

THE PENNSYLVANIA RAILROAD
STANDARD
4, 5 AND 6 POST
TIMBER TRESTLE BRIDGES - OPEN DECK
SHEET 1 OF 3
STANDARD 79301-B, APRIL 1925

Redrawn from original PRR drawings by Jeff Scherb

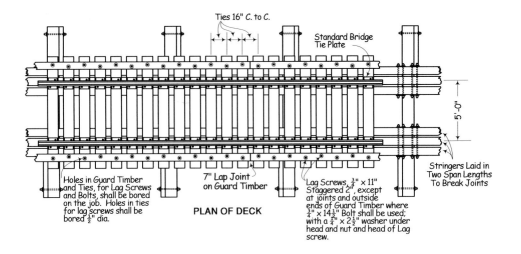

Ties 16" C. to C.

Standard Bridge Tie Plate

5'-0"

Holes in Guard Timber and Ties, for Lag Screws and Bolts, shall be bored on the job. Holes in ties for lag screws shall be bored ½" dia.

7" Lap Joint on Guard Timber

PLAN OF DECK

Lag Screws, ¾" × 11" Staggered 2", except at joints and outside ends of Guard Timber where ¾" × 14½" Bolt shall be used; with a ¾" × 2½" washer under head and nut and head of Lag screw.

Stringers Laid in Two Span Lengths To Break Joints

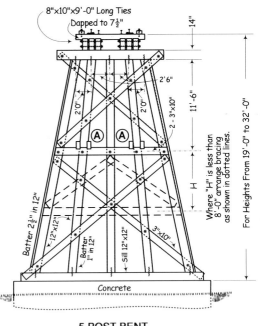

8"×10"×9'-0" Long Ties
Dapped to 7½"

14"

2'6"

2'-0"   2'-0"

2 - 3"×10"

11'-6"

(A) (A)

Batter 2½" in 12"

12"×12"

Batter 1" in 12"

Sill 12"×12"

3"×10"

H

Where "H" is less than 8'-0" arrange bracing as shown in dotted lines.

For Heights From 19'-0" to 32'-0"

Concrete

5 POST BENT
15'-0" C. to C. of Bents

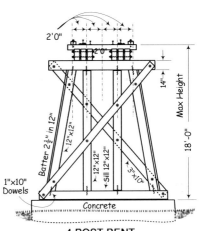

2'0"

2'0"

14"

Batter 2½" in 12"

12"×12"

12"×12"

Sill 12"×12"

3"×10"

Max Height

18'-0"

1"×10" Dowels

Concrete

4 POST BENT
10'-0" and 12'-0" C. to C. of Bents
SAME BRACING SHALL BE USED
ON 5 AND 6 POST BENTS
11'-0" TO 18'-0" HIGH

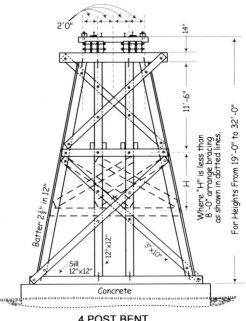

2'0"

14"

11'-6"

Batter 2½" in 12"

12"×12"

3"×10"

Sill 12"×12"

H

Where "H" is less than 8'-0" arrange bracing as shown in dotted lines.

For Heights From 19'-0" to 32'-0"

Concrete

4 POST BENT
10'-0" and 12'-0" C. to C. of Bents

THE PENNSYLVANIA RAILROAD
STANDARD
4, 5 AND 6 POST
TIMBER TRESTLE BRIDGES - OPEN DECK
SHEET 2 OF 3

STANDARD 79301-B, APRIL 1925

Redrawn from original PRR drawings by Jeff Scherb

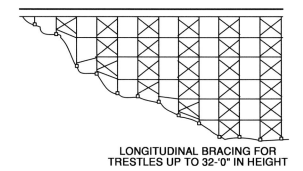

LONGITUDINAL BRACING FOR TRESTLES UP TO 32-'0" IN HEIGHT

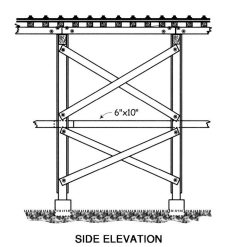

6"x10"

SIDE ELEVATION

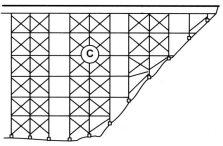

LONGITUDINAL BRACING FOR TRESTLES FROM 32-'0" TO 71'-0" IN HEIGHT

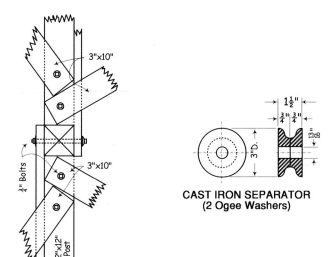

3"x10"

3"x10"

¾" Bolts

12"x12" Post

DETAIL C

CAST IRON SEPARATOR
(2 Ogee Washers)

1½"

¾" ¾"

3"D.

13/16"

Span C. to C. of Bents	Dimensions of Stringers
10'-0" to 12'-0"	3 Pcs. 10"x16" Per Rail
13'-0" to 14'-0"	3 Pcs. 10"x18" Per Rail
15'-0"	3 Pcs. 10"x20" Per Rail

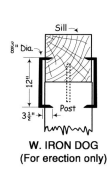

Sill

⅜" Dia.

12"

3½"

Post

W. IRON DOG
(For erection only)

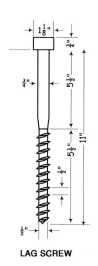

1⅛"

¾"

¾"

5½"

5½"

¼"

11"

½"

LAG SCREW

THE PENNSYLVANIA RAILROAD
STANDARD
4, 5 AND 6 POST
TIMBER TRESTLE BRIDGES - OPEN DECK
SHEET 3 OF 3
STANDARD 79301-B, APRIL 1925

Redrawn from original PRR drawings by Jeff Scherb

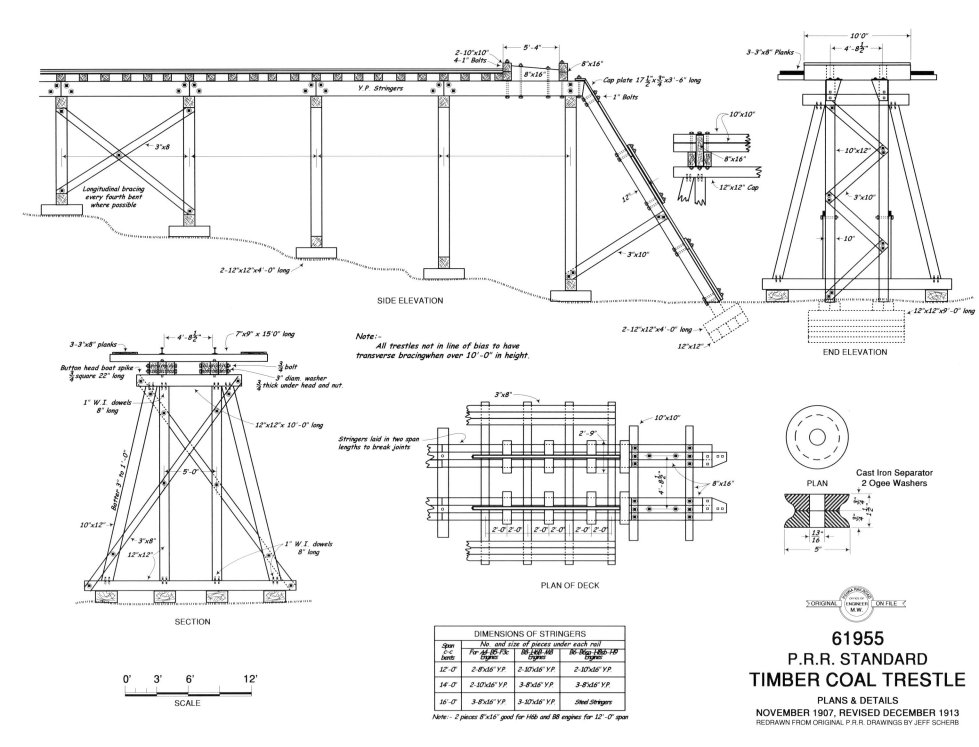

SIDE ELEVATION

END ELEVATION

SECTION

PLAN OF DECK

PLAN

Cast Iron Separator
2 Ogee Washers

Note:-
All trestles not in line of bias to have transverse bracingwhen over 10'-0" in height.

DIMENSIONS OF STRINGERS

Span c-c bents	No. and size of pieces under each rail		
	For A4-B5-F3c Engines	B8-H6B-M8 Engines	B6-B6sa-H8sb-H9 Engines
12'-0"	2-8"x16" Y.P.	2-10"x16" Y.P.	2-10"x16" Y.P.
14'-0"	2-10"x16" Y.P.	3-8"x16" Y.P.	3-8"x16" Y.P.
16'-0"	3-8"x16" Y.P.	3-10"x16" Y.P.	Steel Stringers

Note:- 2 pieces 8"x16" good for H6b and B8 engines for 12'-0" span

SCALE

61955
P.R.R. STANDARD
TIMBER COAL TRESTLE

PLANS & DETAILS
NOVEMBER 1907, REVISED DECEMBER 1913
REDRAWN FROM ORIGINAL P.R.R. DRAWINGS BY JEFF SCHERB

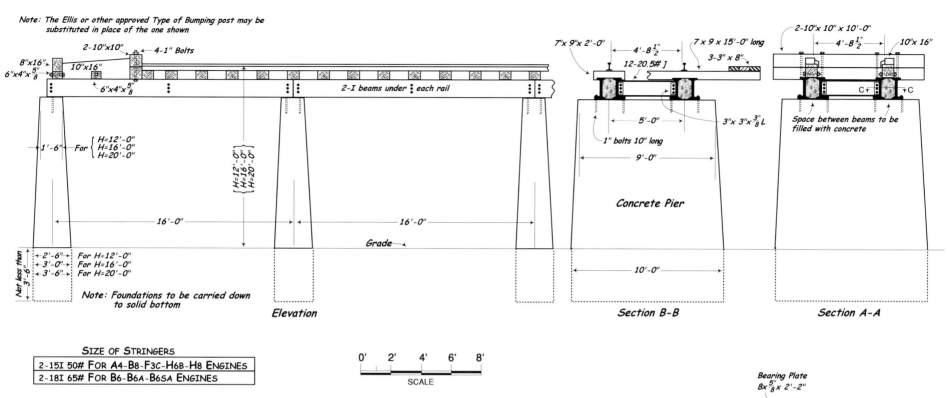

Note: The Ellis or other approved Type of Bumping post may be substituted in place of the one shown

2-10"x10"   4-1" Bolts

8"x16"
10"x16"
6"x4"x⅝

6"x4"x⅝

2-I beams under each rail

1'-6"   For {H=12'-0" / H=16'-0" / H=20'-0"}

{H=12'-0" / H=16'-0" / H=20'-0"}

16'-0"   16'-0"

Grade

Not less than 3'-6"

2'-6"   For H=12'-0"
3'-0"   For H=16'-0"
3'-6"   For H=20'-0"

Note: Foundations to be carried down to solid bottom

Elevation

7'x 9"x 2'-0"   7 x 9 x 15'-0" long

4'-8½"   3-3" x 8"

12-20.5# J

1" bolts 10" long   3"x 3"x ⅜ L

5'-0"

9'-0"

Concrete Pier

10'-0"

Section B-B

2-10"x 10" x 10'-0"

4'-8½"   10"x 16"

C ← → C

Space between beams to be filled with concrete

Section A-A

SIZE OF STRINGERS

| 2-15I 50# FOR A4-B8-F3C-H6B-H8 ENGINES |
| 2-18I 65# FOR B6-B6A-B6SA ENGINES |

0'   2'   4'   6'   8'

SCALE

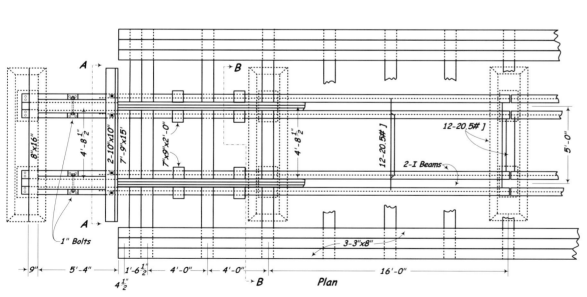

A   B

8"x16"
4'-8½"
2-10"x10"
7'-9"x15'
7'x9"x2'-0"
4'-8½"
12-20.5# J
12-20.5# J
2-I Beams
5'-0"

A

1" Bolts

A

9"   5'-4"   1'-6½"   4'-0"   4'-0"   16'-0"
4½"   B
3-3"x8"   Plan

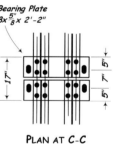

Bearing Plate
8x⅝x 2'-2"

17"   5"

7"

5"

PLAN AT C-C

61957
P.R.R. STANDARD
CONCRETE AND STEEL
COAL TRESTLE
NOVEMBER 1908, REVISED JANUARY 1914
REDRAWN FROM ORIGINAL P.R.R. DRAWINGS BY JEFF SCHERB

SIGNALS

P.R.R. Standard Signals, Aspects and Indications

THE PENNSYLVANIA BECAME the operator of the first block system in the United States in 1871 with the acquisition of the Camden and Amboy Railroad, the main rail link between Philadelphia and New York. A serious accident on this line in 1865 led Camden and Amboy vice president Ashbel Welch to implement a block system on the road, following the lead of the railroads in Great Britain, where block systems were becoming increasingly common. The first section of blocks came into use between Trenton and Kensington. There were six blocks, averaging five miles in length. The blocks were controlled through the telegraph offices in the stations. By 1867, the block system extended through to Jersey City.

The earliest signaling for the block system used two aspects, white to indicate block clear, and red to indicate stop. At each station, block occupancy was tracked through the use of a pegboard, with the operator inserting pegs in the board when a train entered a block. Normally, signals indicated stop. When a train was 1/2 mile from the station, the engineer would whistle, and if the block ahead were clear, the block operator would display the clear signal, allowing the train to proceed.

By the time of the Centennial Exposition of 1876 in Philadelphia, the Pennsylvania had begun to adopt the block system for general use. Blocks were generally 5-6 miles long, and block stations were housed in octagonal signal cabins (see pp. 13-14). The signalman occupied the second story of these attractive structures.

By the 1880s, the crude signal lights used in the early block systems were generally replaced by semaphores, and a third aspect (green) was added. Initially, green indicated Permissive-Block, which allowed a freight train to follow another freight train into a block. In 1917, to improve visibility, green replaced white as the clear aspect, and yellow became the Permissive color. According to one account, green replaced white as a fail-safe — with all aspects being a color, a signal showing a white aspect would indicate a problem, such as a broken or missing lens, perhaps destroyed by vandalism, and would indicate that an engineer should stop and investigate. Prior to this color change, a broken lens showing white would be indistinguishable from a proper white indication, which could lead to accidents.

The first interlocking plant in the United States was put into operation in 1870 at Top-of-the-Hill Junction, near Trenton, on the Camden and Amboy. The Pennsylvania also inherited this in their 1871 acquisition of that road. Common in England by 1860, interlocking ensures the proper synchronization of switches and signals.

Early signaling for interlocking on the Pennsylvania was done by means of semaphores. In the earliest forms, the semaphore only governed through movements on the main track, and also served as block signals, with no indications for the diverging route. Later, multiple semaphores on the same pole were used, although placements of the semaphores on the pole weren't standardized, as they were later, when the high-speed route would be the topmost arm. In earlier forms, the engineer was required to know which semaphore controlled which route.

On busy lines, it was desirable to have a larger number of blocks, so more trains could occupy the mainline simultaneously. In most cases, interlocking signals also served as block signals to simplify the signaling and to provide for more frequent blocks on busy mainlines. Each interlocking plant and block boundary had a signal tower and was manned. The manual nature of this system became very expensive on lesser-used branchlines, but lengthening the blocks so that fewer block operators would be necessary wasn't a good solution either, since it limited the traffic a line could handle. The solution the Pennsylvania came up with was the Block-Limit station. This was an unmanned block boundary, indicated by a Block-Limit signal (p. 55). The train was required to stop at these signals, unless permitted to continue without stopping by a Train Order. Telephone boxes (p. 60) were placed at these signals, and the engineer was required to call ahead for clearance to proceed. Accompanying the block limit signals were Approach Block-Limit signs (p. 55), giving the engineer warning to stop ahead at the Block-Limit signal.

The well-known Pennsylvania standard position-light signals were first used in 1915 on the Main Line between Paoli and Overbrook, near Philadelphia. Developed by Arthur Holley Rudd, the company's Signal Engineer, these original signals had four white lights in a row, and were called "tombstone" signals because of their resemblance to that item. A number of different light and lens configurations were tried over the next few years until about 1921, when the three-light system still in use today was developed. The Pennsylvania's signal engineers had determined by that time that rows of three lights were all that were needed to eliminate misinterpretation of the signal due to bulb outages or distance. By 1935, 71 percent of the signals had been replaced with position lights, and by the 1940s, 97 percent of the Pennsylvania's main and secondary lines had been converted to three-light position-light signals.

Dwarf position-light signals were common in low-speed operation areas, such as yards, and consisted of a single pivot light with three position lights. Lenses were frosted to limit the distance they could be viewed to eliminate the possibility of confusion with high signals.

Position-light signals were used only for speed signaling, not route signaling. Interlocking and route signaling remained controlled by semaphores well into the second half of the twentieth century.

Several mail cranes have been included in this section of the book as well — while they are not signals, they are more closely related to signaling equipment than they are to the other categories in the book. When mail service was a significant part of the railroad's service to a community, most passenger trains included a Railway Post Office (RPO) car. When the train stopped at a station, bags of mail could be loaded or unloaded. If the train didn't stop at a station, mail pouches were unloaded by tossing them off the train to the station platform. A moving train picked up mail by catching a mail pouch held in a mail crane with a hook attached to the side of the RPO.

The Office of the General Superintendent of Railway Mail Service (part of the Post Office) published standard specifications for mail cranes as early as September 1886. Initially, cranes were of wooden construction (p. 61), but around the turn of the century, railroad equipment suppliers began introducing metal cranes. These cranes were much more durable than the earlier wooden cranes, which had a life expectancy of only about five years. ▼

Rule 275: STOP

Indication: Stop

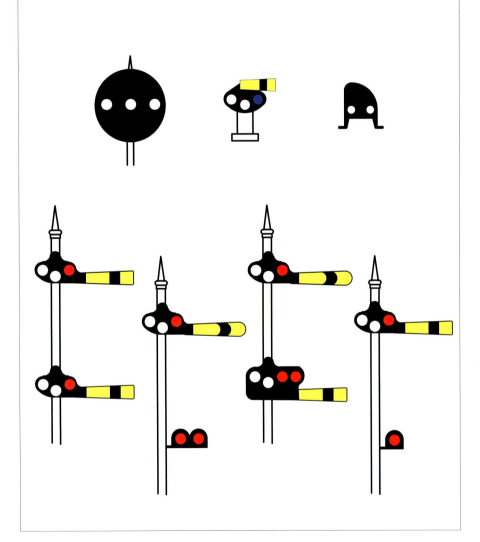

Rule 276: STOP-AND-PROCEED

Indication: Stop, then proceed in accordance with Rule 509 or Rule 660.

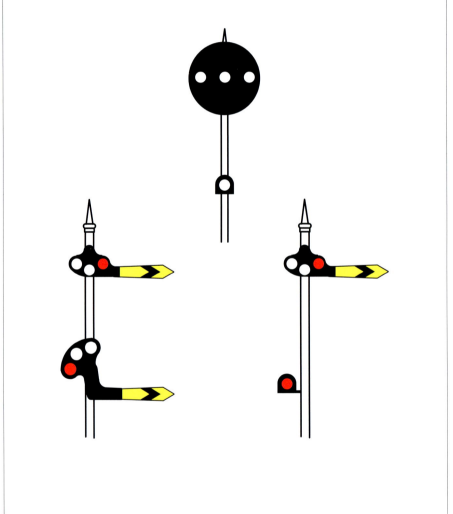

Rule 277: GRADE SIGNAL

Indication: For tonnage freight trains proceed not exceeding 15 miles per hour, expecting to find a train in the block, broken rail, obstruction or switch not properly set. For other trains, then proceed in accordance with rule 509.

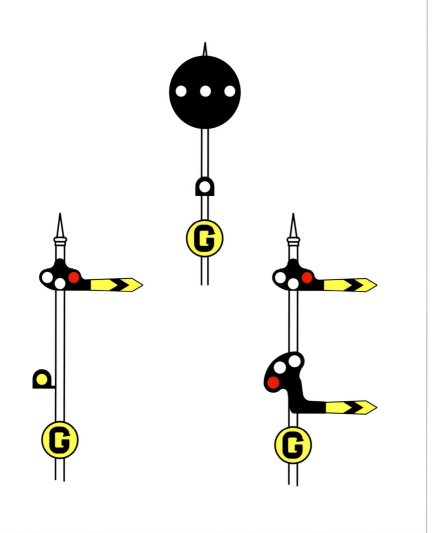

Rule 278: CAUTION-SLOW-SPEED

Indication: Proceed at not exceeding 15 miles per hour with caution prepared to stop short of train or obstruction.

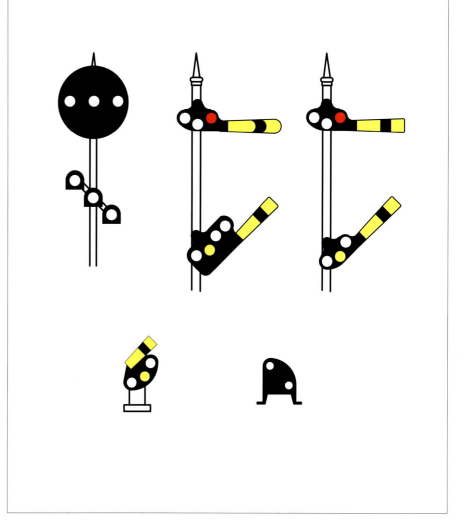

Rule 279: SLOW-SPEED

Indication: Proceed at not exceeding 15 miles per hour
prepared to stop at next signal

Rule 280: PERMISSIVE-BLOCK

Indication: For passenger trains stop and report in
accordance with Rule 362 or Rule 462.
For other trains proceed with caution prepared to
stop short of train or obstruction.

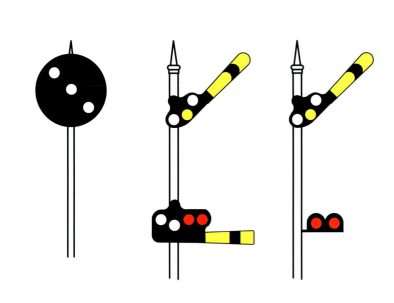

Rule 281: CLEAR-SLOW-SPEED

Indication: Proceed at not exceeding 15 miles per hour.

Rule 282: CAUTION

Indication: Approach next signal prepared to stop. Where a facing switch is connected with the signal, approach that switch prepared to stop. A train exceeding one-half its maximum authorized speed at point involved must at once reduce to not exceeding that speed.

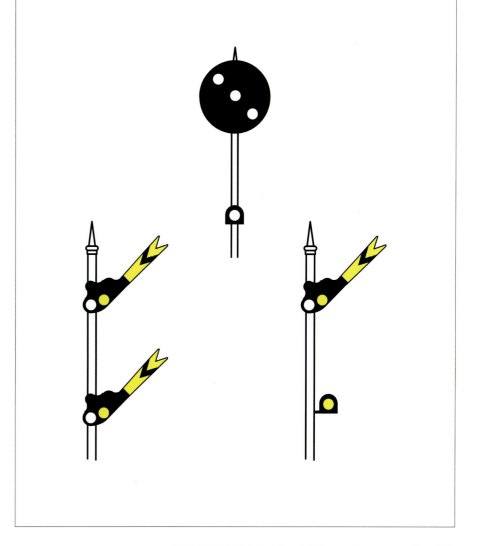

Rule 283: APPROACH

Indication: Approach next signal prepared to stop. A train exceeding one-half its maximum authorized speed at point involved must at once reduce to not exceeding that speed.

Rule 284: APPROACH-RESTRICTING

Indication: Train approach next signal at not exceeding one-half its maximum speed at point involved but not exceeding 30 miles per hour.

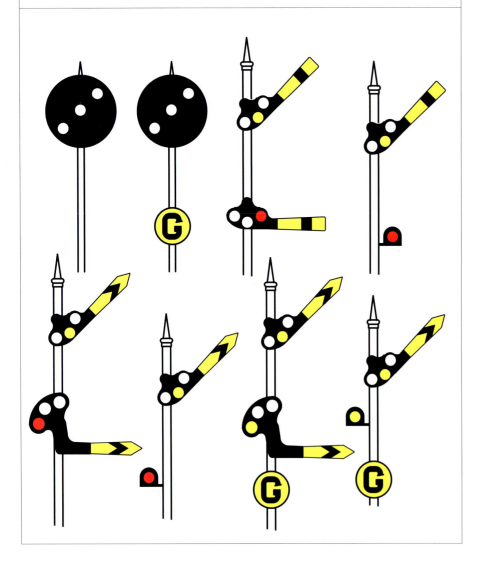

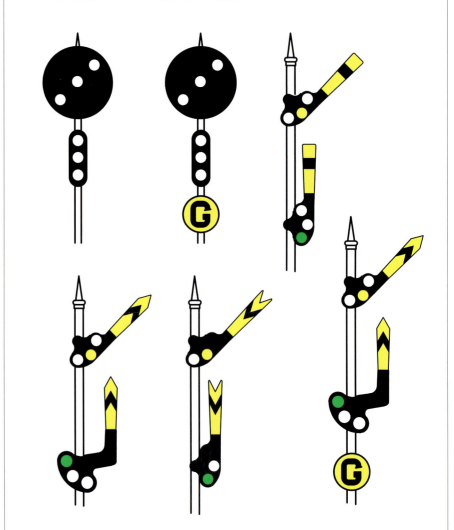

Rule 285: CLEAR-RESTRICTING

Indication: Train proceed at not exceeding one-half its maximum authorized speed at point involved but not exceeding 30 miles per hour.

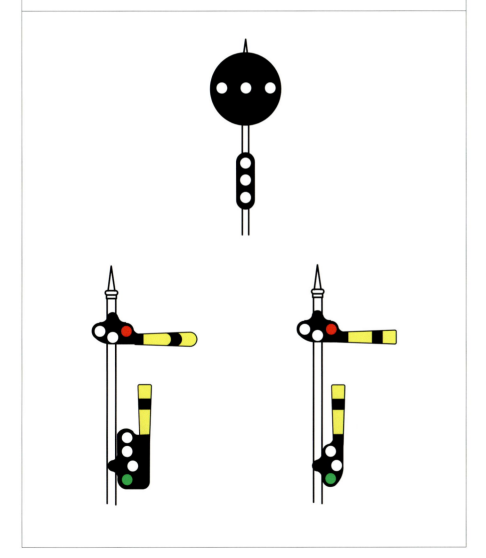

Rule 286: CLEAR-SIGNAL

Indication: Proceed.

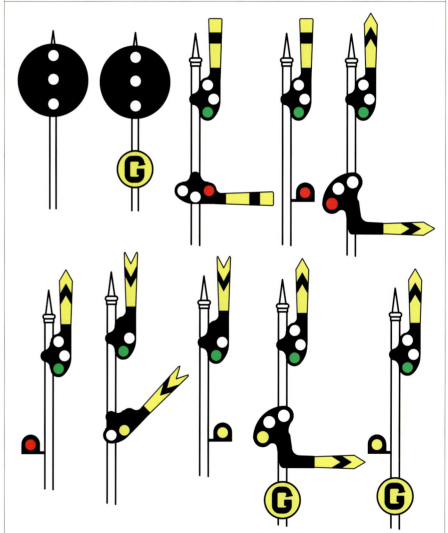

Rule 287: CLEAR-BLOCK

Indication: Proceed-manual or controlled manual block clear.

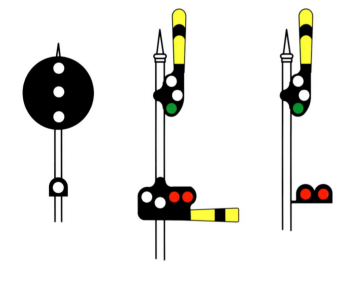

Rule 288: TAKE-SIDING

Indication: Take siding.

SIGNAL ASPECTS

1	2	3	4	5	6	7	8	9	11	12

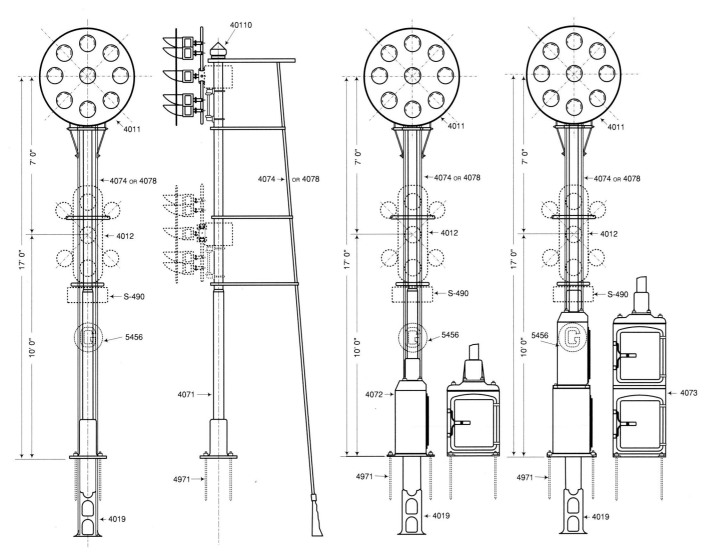

4061 - SIGNAL   4062 - SIGNAL   4063 - SIGNAL

NOTES:-

1. MARKER LIGHT SHALL BE SINGLE LAMP UNIT WITHOUT BACKGROUND BUT WITH NECESSARY FITTINGS FOR ATTACHING TO STANDARD 5" PIPE.

2. SIGNALS SHALL BE COMPLETE WITH HUB, NECESSARY RADIAL PIPING, JUNCTION BOX, BACKGROUND, LAMP UNITS AS ORDERED, BOLTS, ETC., FOR INSTALLATION, EXCEPT FOUNDATION BOLTS WHICH SHALL BE ORDERED FROM STANDARD PLAN S-497

3. ALL OPENINGS IN BACKGROUND SHALL BE CUT, THOSE NOT USED SHALL BE COVERED WITH IRON DISCS.

4. FOR WIRING OF TERMINALS SEE STANDARD PLAN S-858

5. WHERE SIGNAL IS LOCATED BETWEEN TRACKS, THE TRACKS SHALL BE NOT LESS THAN 20'-0" CENTERS.

6. WHEN ORDERING SIGNALS SPECIFY FIGURE NUMBER, TOGETHER WITH ASPECTS DESIRED.

7. CIRCULAR BACKGROUND SHALL BE FURNISHED FOR TOP ARM OF ALL SIGNALS.

8. BACKGROUND 4012 SHALL BE FURNISHED FOR BOTTOM ARM, ONLY WHENE ASPECT No. 6 OR No. 8 IS TO BE DISPLAYED.

9. WHEN NO DETAILED REFERENCE IS SHOWN, THE MANUFACTURER'S STANDARD APPARATUS SHALL BE FURNISHED.

10. FOUNDATION BOLT HOLES IN BASE CASTINGS SHALL BE FILLED WITH PUTTY AFTER INSTALLATION.

PENNSYLVANIA SYSTEM

STANDARD
SIGNALS
POSITION LIGHT

DRAWING #S-406-A, MAY 1926

Redrawn from original PRR drawings
by Jeff Scherb

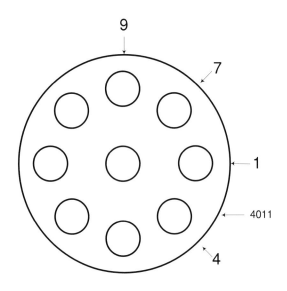

SIGNAL A

ORDER NO.	SIGNAL ASPECTS
4051	1
4052	4
4053	7
4054	7 - 9
4055	1 - 9
4056	4 - 9
4057	1 - 7 - 9
4058	4 - 7 - 9
4059	1 - 4 - 7 - 9
40510	1 - 4 - 9
40511	1 - 7
40512	4 - 7
40513	1 - 4 - 7
40514	1 - 4

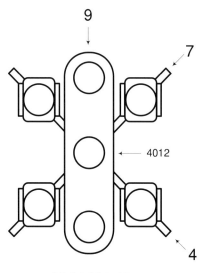

SIGNAL B

ORDER NO.	SIGNAL ASPECTS
40517	9
40518	7 - 9
40519	4 - 9
40520	4 - 7 - 9

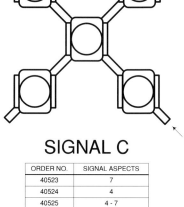

SIGNAL C

ORDER NO.	SIGNAL ASPECTS
40523	7
40524	4
40525	4 - 7

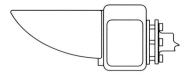

MARKER

ORDER NO.	SINGLE UNIT
40528	COMPLETE FOR ATTACHING TO 5" STANDARD MAST
40529	COMPLETE FOR ATTACHING TO 11/4" LORICATED PIPE

NOTE:-

SIGNALS SHALL BE COMPLETE WITH HUB, NECESSARY RADIAL PIPING, JUNCTION BOX, FLEXIBLE AND WIRING BETWEEN JUNCTION BOX AND LIGHT UNITS, BACKGROUND (AS SHOWN), BOLTS ETC., FOR ATTACHING TO 5" STANDARD MAST, UNLESS OTHERWISE SPECIFIED.

PENNSYLVANIA SYSTEM

STANDARD
SIGNALS
POSITION LIGHT

DRAWING #S-405-A, AUGUST 1935

Redrawn from original PRR drawings
by Jeff Scherb

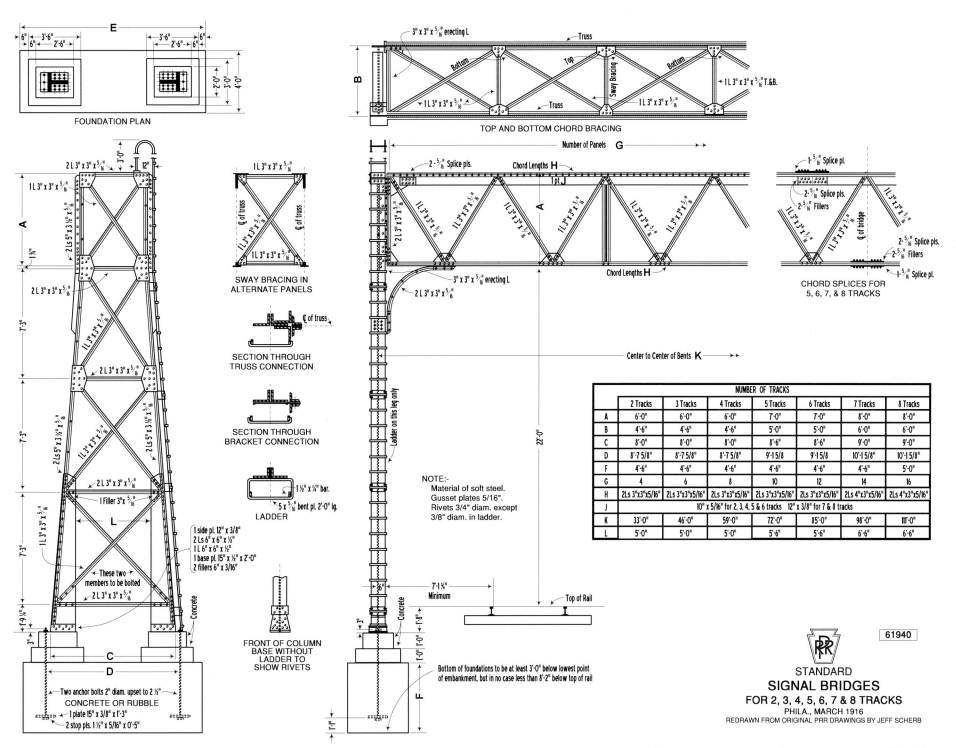

FOUNDATION PLAN

TOP AND BOTTOM CHORD BRACING

SWAY BRACING IN ALTERNATE PANELS

SECTION THROUGH TRUSS CONNECTION

SECTION THROUGH BRACKET CONNECTION

LADDER

FRONT OF COLUMN BASE WITHOUT LADDER TO SHOW RIVETS

CHORD SPLICES FOR 5, 6, 7, & 8 TRACKS

NOTE:-
Material of soft steel.
Gusset plates 5/16".
Rivets 3/4" diam. except 3/8" diam. in ladder.

Two anchor bolts 2" diam. upset to 2 ½"
CONCRETE OR RUBBLE
1 plate 15" x 3/8" x 1'-3"
2 stop pls. 1 ½" x 5/16" x 0'-5"

1 side pl. 12" x 3/8"
2 Ls 6" x 6" x ½"
1 L 6" x 6" x ½"
1 base pl. 15" x ½" x 2'-0"
2 fillers 6" x 3/16"

These two members to be bolted
2 L 3" x 3" x 5/16"

Bottom of foundations to be at least 3'-0" below lowest point of embankment, but in no case less than 8'-2" below top of rail

NUMBER OF TRACKS							
	2 Tracks	3 Tracks	4 Tracks	5 Tracks	6 Tracks	7 Tracks	8 Tracks
A	6'-0"	6'-0"	6'-0"	7'-0"	7'-0"	8'-0"	8'-0"
B	4'-6"	4'-6"	4'-6"	5'-0"	5'-0"	6'-0"	6'-0"
C	8'-0"	8'-0"	8'-0"	8'-6"	8'-6"	9'-0"	9'-0"
D	8'-7 5/8"	8'-7 5/8"	8'-7 5/8"	9'-1 5/8"	9'-1 5/8"	10'-1 5/8"	10'-1 5/8"
F	4'-6"	4'-6"	4'-6"	4'-6"	4'-6"	4'-6"	5'-0"
G	4	6	8	10	12	14	16
H	2Ls 3"x3"x5/16"	2Ls 3"x3"x5/16"	2Ls 3"x3"x5/16"	2Ls 3"x3"x5/16"	2Ls 3"x3"x5/16"	2Ls 4"x3"x5/16"	2Ls 4"x3"x5/16"
J			10" x 5/16" for 2, 3, 4, 5 & 6 tracks			12" x 3/8" for 7 & 8 tracks	
K	33'-0"	46'-0"	59'-0"	72'-0"	85'-0"	98'-0"	111'-0"
L	5'-0"	5'-0"	5'-0"	5'-6"	5'-6"	6'-6"	6'-6"

61940

STANDARD
SIGNAL BRIDGES
FOR 2, 3, 4, 5, 6, 7 & 8 TRACKS
PHILA., MARCH 1916
REDRAWN FROM ORIGINAL PRR DRAWINGS BY JEFF SCHERB

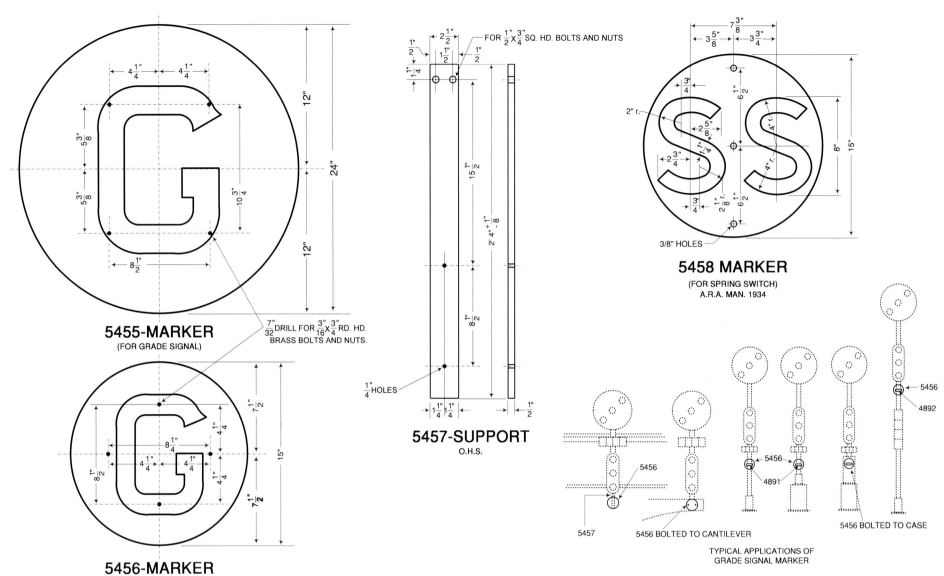

5455-MARKER
(FOR GRADE SIGNAL)

$\frac{7}{32}$ DRILL FOR $\frac{3}{16}$ X $\frac{3}{4}$ RD. HD. BRASS BOLTS AND NUTS.

5456-MARKER
(FOR GRADE SIGNAL)

FOR $\frac{1}{2}$ X $\frac{3}{4}$ SQ. HD. BOLTS AND NUTS

$\frac{1}{4}$ HOLES

5457-SUPPORT
O.H.S.

5458 MARKER
(FOR SPRING SWITCH)
A.R.A. MAN. 1934

3/8" HOLES

5456

4892

5456

4891

5457

5456 BOLTED TO CANTILEVER

5456 BOLTED TO CASE

TYPICAL APPLICATIONS OF
GRADE SIGNAL MARKER

NOTES:-
A- GRADE SIGNAL:
1. MARKERS SHALL BE MADE OF #16 U.S. STD. GAUGE OPEN HEARTH ENAMELING STEEL AND ENAMELED WITH NOT LESS THAN THREE (3) COATS OF VITREOUS ENAMEL.
2. LETTER "G" SHALL BE ENAMELED, BLACK ON A YELLOW ENAMELED BACKGROUND
3. BACK OF MARKER SHALL BE ENAMELED BLACK
4. LETTER "G" FOR 5455 SHALL BE 14" HIGH.
   LETTER "G" FOR 5456 SHALL BE 10" HIGH.
5. MARKER 5455 SHALL BE USED ON OLD STYLE BRIDGE AND CANTILEVER SIGNALS ONLY.
6. SUPPORT 5457 SHALL BE PAINTED BLACK

B - SPRING SWITCH:
1. MARKERS SHALL BE MADE OF #12 U.S. STD GAUGE (.105") SHEET STEEL AND ENAMELED, BOTH SIDES WHITE WITH BLACK LETTERS, SEMI-GLOSS FINISH.
2. MARKER TO BE SET AT RIGHT ANGLES TO TRACK AND MAY BE MOUNTED ON SWITCH STAND OR SEPARATE POST.

PENNSYLVANIA SYSTEM

PRR

STANDARD
MARKERS
FOR SWITCHES AND SIGNALS
STANDARD #S-545-F, JUNE 1927
Redrawn from original PRR drawings
by Jeff Scherb

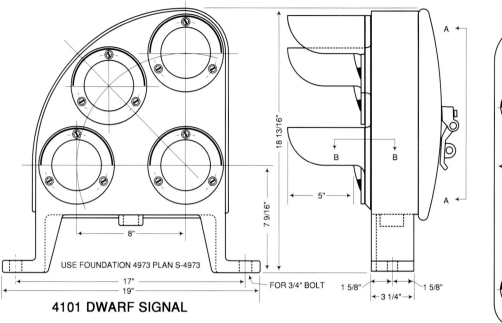

4101 DWARF SIGNAL

USE FOUNDATION 4973 PLAN S-4973

18 13/16"
7 9/16"
8"
17"
19"
FOR 3/4" BOLT
5"
1 5/8" 1 5/8"
3 1/4"

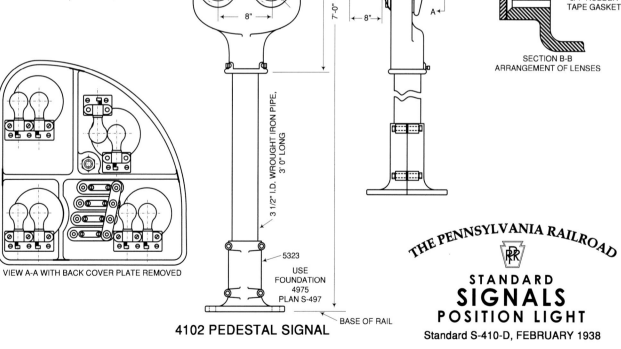

12"
8"
16"
2'-2"
4' 1 15/16"
7'-0"
8"
8"

A ──► ◄── A
B   B
A ──► ◄── A
B   B

VIEW A-A WITH BACK COVER PLATE REMOVED

3 1/2" I.D. WROUGHT IRON PIPE, 3' 0" LONG

5323
USE FOUNDATION 4975 PLAN S-497

BASE OF RAIL

4102 PEDESTAL SIGNAL

1/8" CORK GASKET

2 1/4" FOCAL LENGTH

4832

4877

4864

3/4" RUBBER TAPE GASKET

SECTION B-B
ARRANGEMENT OF LENSES

NOTE:-
1. WHEN ORDERING SIGNALS, SPECIFY FIGURE NUMBER, TOGETHER WITH ASPECTS ORDERED.
2. SIGNALS SHALL BE FURNISHED COMPLETE AS SHOWN WITHOUT LAMPS.
3. WHEN INSTALLING, SIGNALS SHALL BE WIRED IN ACCORDANCE WITH STANDARD PLAN S-858.
4. ALL INDICATIONS NOT USED SHALL BE BLANKED.

1	4	5	7

ASPECTS FOR SIGNAL 4101

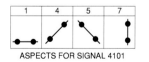

1	2	4	5	9	10	11	12

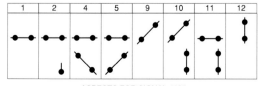

ASPECTS FOR SIGNAL 4102

THE PENNSYLVANIA RAILROAD

PRR

STANDARD
SIGNALS
POSITION LIGHT

Standard S-410-D, FEBRUARY 1938

Redrawn from original PRR drawings
by Jeff Scherb

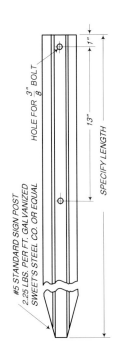

#5 STANDARD SIGN POST
2.25 LBS. PER FT. GALVANIZED
SWEET'S STEEL CO. OR EQUAL

HOLE FOR 3/8" BOLT

1"

13"

SPECIFY LENGTH

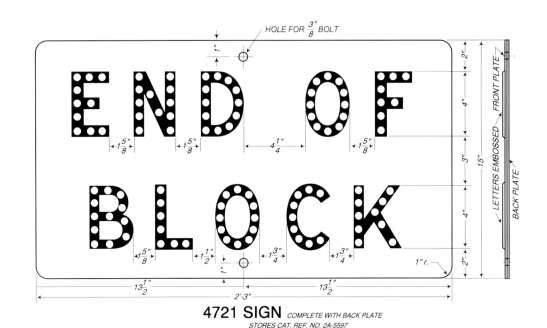

HOLE FOR 3/8" BOLT

1"

END OF BLOCK

1 5/8" 1 5/8" 4 1/4" 1 5/8"

1 5/8" 1 1/2" 1 3/4" 1 3/4"

1"

2" 4" 3" 4" 2"

15"

LETTERS EMBOSSED
FRONT PLATE
BACK PLATE

1" r.

13 1/2" 13 1/2"

2'-3"

4721 SIGN
COMPLETE WITH BACK PLATE
STORES CAT. REF. NO. 2A-5597

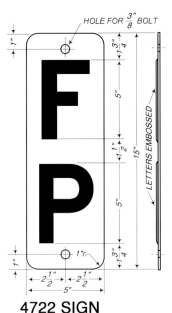

HOLE FOR 3/8" BOLT

1" 3" 1 1/4"

F
P

1 1/2" 5" 5" 1 1/4"

15"

LETTERS EMBOSSED

1" 3" 1 1/4"

2 1/2" 2 1/2"

5"

4722 SIGN
STORES CAT. REF. NO. 2A-5598

4723 SIGN POST *HIGH CARBON RAIL STEEL.*
STORES CAT. REF. NO. 2A-5599

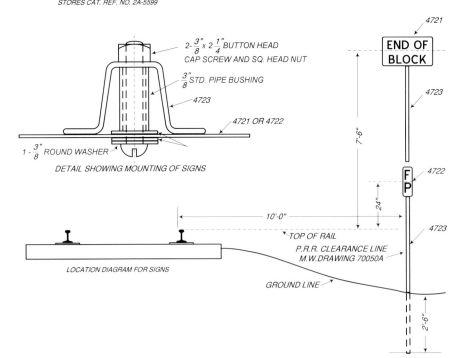

2 - 3/8" x 2 1/4" BUTTON HEAD
CAP SCREW AND SQ. HEAD NUT

3/8" STD. PIPE BUSHING

4723

4721 OR 4722

1 - 3/8" ROUND WASHER

DETAIL SHOWING MOUNTING OF SIGNS

4721

4723

7'-6"

F P 4722

24"

4723

10'-0"

TOP OF RAIL

P.R.R. CLEARANCE LINE
M.W. DRAWING 70050A

GROUND LINE

2'-6"

LOCATION DIAGRAM FOR SIGNS

NOTES:-
1. MATERIAL FOR FRONT PLATE AND BACK PLATE OF SIGN 4721 AND SIGN PLATE OF SIGN 4722 SHALL BE #16 GAUGE GALVANNEALED STEEL, OR STEEL PARKERIZED AFTER FABRICATION. LETTERS ON BOTH SIDES OF SIGN SHALL BE EMBOSSED.
2. FOR SIGN 4721, THE COLOR OF BACKGROUND AND BACK OF FRONT PLATE SHALL BE BLACK BAKED-ON ENAMEL. COLOR OF LETTERS SHALL BE WHITE BAKED-ON ENAMEL. FRONT AND BACK OF BACK PLATE SHALL BE BLACK BAKED-ON ENAMEL.
3. FOR SIGN 4722, THE COLOR OF BACKGROUND AND BACK OF SIGN SHALL BE WHITE BAKED-ON ENAMEL. COLOR OF LETTERS SHALL BE BLACK BAKED-ON ENAMEL.
4. REFLECTOR BUTTONS FOR SIGN 4721 SHALL BE ROUND, OF THE PRISMATIC TYPE 1/2" INCH IN DIAMETER, #5 CLEAR STIMSONITE, ALL PLASTIC, MOUNTED BETWEEN FRONT AND BACK PLATES. NUMBER OF BUTTONS AS INDICATED.
5. MANUFACTURER OF SIGNS SHALL FURNISH SIGN 4721 OR SIGN 4722 ONLY.
6. LETTERS OF SIGN SHALL BE PROPORTIONED IN ACCORDANCE WITH UNITED STATES PUBLIC ROADS ADMINISTRATION, FEDERAL WORKS AGENCY DESIGN, SERIES D, BOOKLET P-3378.
7. SIGN 4722 SHALL BE LOCATED, LONGITUDINALLY, 10 FEET BACK OF A POINT, WHERE TRACK CENTERS BETWEEN MAIN TRACK AND TRACK TO WHICH SIGN APPLIES ARE SEPARATED BY AT LEAST 12 FEET 2 INCHES.
8. SIGNS SHALL BE ATTACHED TO SIGN POST 4723 ONLY.
9. SIGN POST 4723 SHALL BE DRIVEN INTO GROUND AT LOCATION SELECTED, AFTER WHICH SIGN 4721 OR SIGN 4722 SHALL BE MOUNTED THEREON AS SHOWN IN DETAIL ON THIS DRAWING.
10. THE 3/8" BUSHING INDICATED IN DETAIL OF MOUNTING, SHALL BE OF SUCH LENGTH THAT SIGN WILL BEAR FIRMLY AGAINST POST, BUT NOT TO BEND SIGN.
11. FRONT AND BACK PLATES OF SIGN 4721 SHALL BE FIRMLY HELD TOGETHER WITH TWELVE 10/24 x 5/16" ALUMINUM ASSEMBLY BOLTS WITH VANDAL RESISTING NUTS.

PENNSYLVANIA SYSTEM

STANDARD
SIGNS
END OF BLOCK AND FOULING POINT
STANDARD #S-472-A, SEPTEMBER 1949
Redrawn from original PRR drawings
by Jeff Scherb

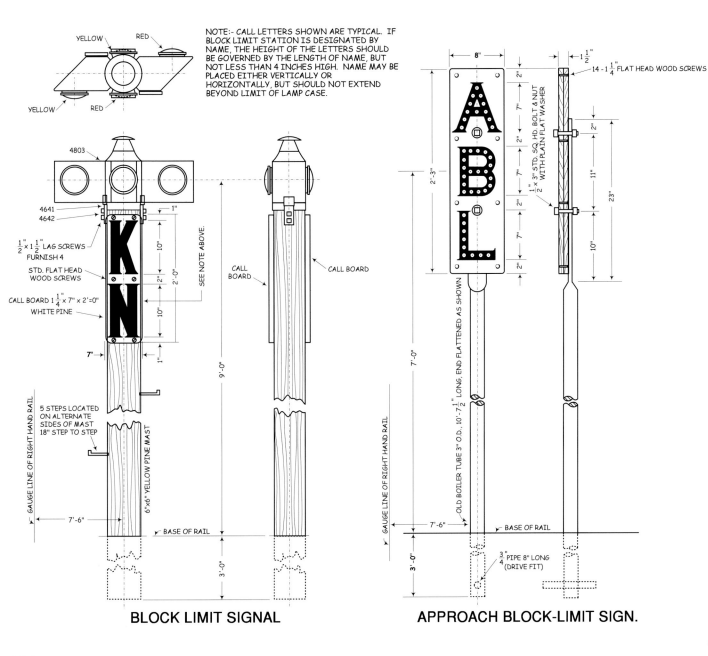

NOTE:- CALL LETTERS SHOWN ARE TYPICAL. IF BLOCK LIMIT STATION IS DESIGNATED BY NAME, THE HEIGHT OF THE LETTERS SHOULD BE GOVERNED BY THE LENGTH OF NAME, BUT NOT LESS THAN 4 INCHES HIGH. NAME MAY BE PLACED EITHER VERTICALLY OR HORIZONTALLY, BUT SHOULD NOT EXTEND BEYOND LIMIT OF LAMP CASE.

YELLOW   RED
YELLOW   RED

4803
4641
4642

$\frac{1}{2}" \times 1\frac{1}{2}"$ LAG SCREWS
FURNISH 4

STD. FLAT HEAD WOOD SCREWS

CALL BOARD $1\frac{1}{4}" \times 7" \times 2'=0"$
WHITE PINE

SEE NOTE ABOVE.

CALL BOARD

CALL BOARD

1"
10"
2"
10"
7"
1"
9'-0"

GAUGE LINE OF RIGHT HAND RAIL

5 STEPS LOCATED ON ALTERNATE SIDES OF MAST 18" STEP TO STEP

6"x6" YELLOW PINE MAST

7'-6"
BASE OF RAIL
3'-0"

BLOCK LIMIT SIGNAL

8"
$1\frac{1}{2}"$
14 - $1\frac{1}{4}"$ FLAT HEAD WOOD SCREWS
2"
7"
2"
7"
2"
7"
2"
2'-3"

$\frac{1}{2}" \times 3"$ STD. SQ. HD. BOLT & NUT WITH PLAIN FLAT WASHER

2"
11"
23"
10"

OLD BOILER TUBE 3" O.D., 10'-$7\frac{1}{2}"$ LONG, END FLATTENED AS SHOWN

7'-0"

GAUGE LINE OF RIGHT HAND RAIL

7'-6"
BASE OF RAIL
3'-0"

$\frac{3}{4}"$ PIPE 8" LONG (DRIVE FIT)

APPROACH BLOCK-LIMIT SIGN.

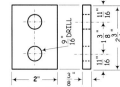

2"
$\frac{9}{16}"$ DRILL
$\frac{11}{16}"$
$\frac{3}{8}"$
$1\frac{3}{8}"$
$2\frac{3}{4}"$
$\frac{11}{16}"$
$\frac{3}{8}"$

4642 FILLER
O.H.S.
STORES CAT. REF. No. 2A-4109.

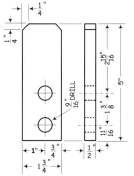

$\frac{1}{4}"$
$\frac{1}{4}"$
$\frac{9}{16}"$ DRILL
$\frac{11}{16}"$
$2\frac{5}{16}"$
5"
1"
$\frac{3}{4}"$
$1\frac{3}{4}"$
$\frac{1}{2}"$

4641 LAMP BRACKET
O.H.S.
STORES CAT. REF. No. 2A-384.

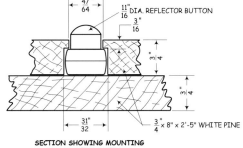

$\frac{47}{64}"$
$\frac{11}{16}"$ DIA. REFLECTOR BUTTON
$\frac{3}{16}"$
$\frac{3}{4}"$
$\frac{3}{4}"$
$\frac{31}{32}"$
$\frac{3}{4}" \times 8" \times 2'-5"$ WHITE PINE

SECTION SHOWING MOUNTING OF REFLECTOR BUTTONS

NOTES:-

BLOCK-LIMIT SIGNAL
1. PAINT FRONT, BACK AND EDGES OF CALL BOARD BLACK, AND THE LETTERS WHITE.
2. PAINT MAST AND LAMP CASE BLACK.
3. LETTERS SHALL BE CONDENSED TYPE IN ACCORDANCE WITH PLAN No. 78000-C.

APPROACH BLOCK-LIMIT SIGNAL
4. PAINT FACE OF SIGN, CLEVELAND BUFF WITH LETTERS BLACK.
5. PAINT EDGES & BACK OF SIGN AND PIPE POST BLACK.
6. LETTERS SHALL BE FULL WIDTH IN ACCORDANCE WITH PLAN No. 78000-C.
7. REFLECTOR BUTTONS SHALL BE CLEAR (COLORLESS) SIMILAR TO TYPE 2A "REFLEX" BUTTON, PEERLESS MFG. CO.

1 SHEET   **S-464-C**

THE PENNSYLVANIA RAILROAD
STANDARD
BLOCK-LIMIT SIGNAL
AND
APPROACH BLOCK-LIMIT SIGN
OFFICE OF CHIEF ENGINEER, PHILA., PA., JUNE 18, 1943
REDRAWN FROM ORIGINAL P.R.R. DRAWINGS BY JEFF SCHERB

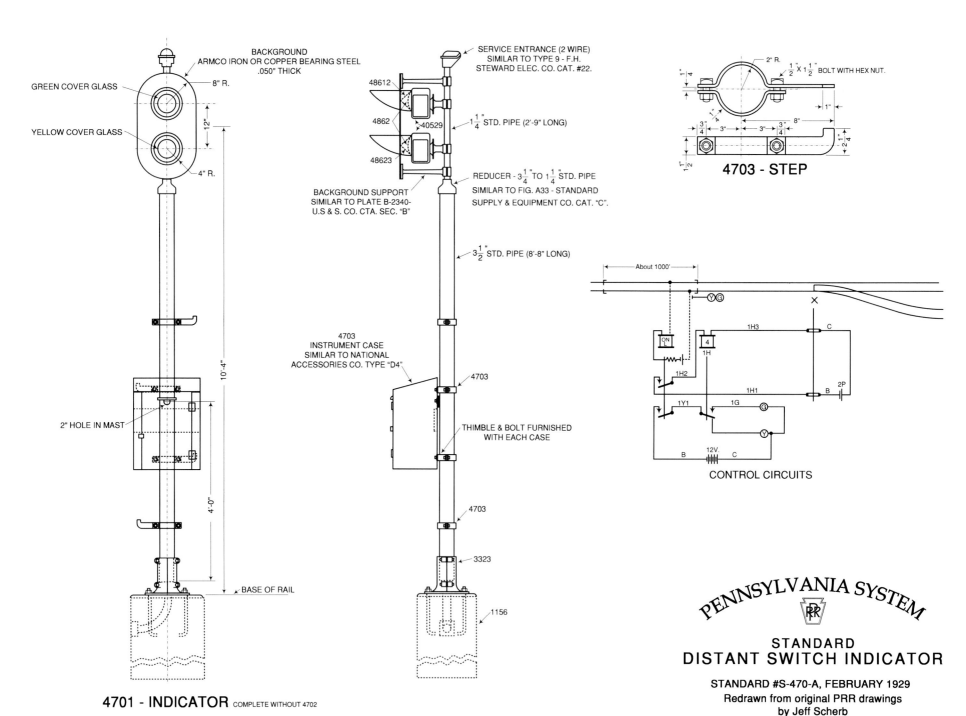

BACKGROUND
ARMCO IRON OR COPPER BEARING STEEL
.050" THICK

GREEN COVER GLASS

8" R.

YELLOW COVER GLASS

12"

4" R.

2" HOLE IN MAST

10'-4"

4'-0"

BASE OF RAIL

4701 - INDICATOR COMPLETE WITHOUT 4702

SERVICE ENTRANCE (2 WIRE)
SIMILAR TO TYPE 9 - F.H.
STEWARD ELEC. CO. CAT. #22.

48612

4862   40529

48623

BACKGROUND SUPPORT
SIMILAR TO PLATE B-2340-
U.S & S. CO. CTA. SEC. "B"

$1\frac{1}{4}$" STD. PIPE (2'-9" LONG)

REDUCER - $3\frac{1}{4}$" TO $1\frac{1}{4}$" STD. PIPE
SIMILAR TO FIG. A33 - STANDARD
SUPPLY & EQUIPMENT CO. CAT. "C".

$3\frac{1}{2}$" STD. PIPE (8'-8" LONG)

4703
INSTRUMENT CASE
SIMILAR TO NATIONAL
ACCESSORIES CO. TYPE "D4"

4703

THIMBLE & BOLT FURNISHED
WITH EACH CASE

4703

3323

1156

2" R.

$\frac{1}{2}$" X $1\frac{1}{2}$" BOLT WITH HEX NUT.

1"
4

1"

$\frac{3}{4}$ 3"   3" $\frac{3}{4}$
1"
4

8"

$\frac{1}{2}$

$2\frac{1}{4}$"

4703 - STEP

About 1000'

Y G

X

ON

4

1H

1H3

C

1H2

1H1

2P

B

1Y1   1G   G

Y

B   12V.   C

CONTROL CIRCUITS

PENNSYLVANIA SYSTEM

PRR

STANDARD
DISTANT SWITCH INDICATOR

STANDARD #S-470-A, FEBRUARY 1929
Redrawn from original PRR drawings
by Jeff Scherb

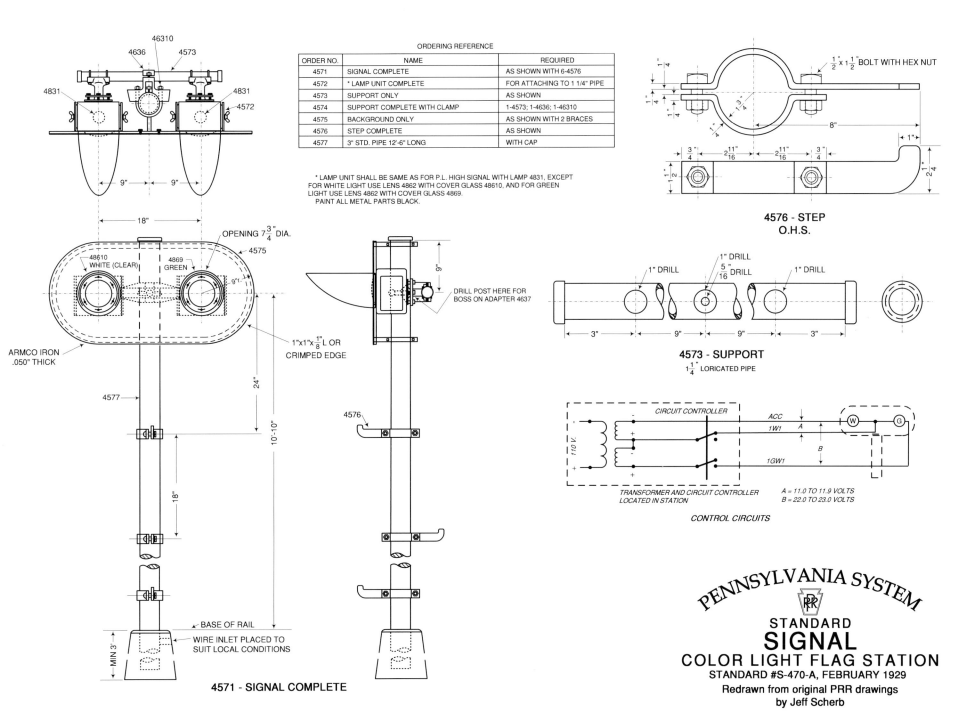

ORDERING REFERENCE

ORDER NO.	NAME	REQUIRED
4571	SIGNAL COMPLETE	AS SHOWN WITH 6-4576
4572	* LAMP UNIT COMPLETE	FOR ATTACHING TO 1 1/4" PIPE
4573	SUPPORT ONLY	AS SHOWN
4574	SUPPORT COMPLETE WITH CLAMP	1-4573; 1-4636; 1-46310
4575	BACKGROUND ONLY	AS SHOWN WITH 2 BRACES
4576	STEP COMPLETE	AS SHOWN
4577	3" STD. PIPE 12'-6" LONG	WITH CAP

* LAMP UNIT SHALL BE SAME AS FOR P.L. HIGH SIGNAL WITH LAMP 4831, EXCEPT FOR WHITE LIGHT USE LENS 4862 WITH COVER GLASS 48610, AND FOR GREEN LIGHT USE LENS 4862 WITH COVER GLASS 4869.
PAINT ALL METAL PARTS BLACK.

46310
4636   4573
4831   4831
4572

9"   9"

18"

OPENING 7 3/4" DIA.
4575
48610 WHITE (CLEAR)
4869 GREEN
9"r.
ARMCO IRON .050" THICK
1"x1"x 1/8 L OR CRIMPED EDGE
4577
24"
10'-10"
18"
BASE OF RAIL
WIRE INLET PLACED TO SUIT LOCAL CONDITIONS
MIN 3'

4571 - SIGNAL COMPLETE

9"
DRILL POST HERE FOR BOSS ON ADAPTER 4637
4576

1/2" x 1 1/2" BOLT WITH HEX NUT
1/4
1/4
1/4
1 3/4
1"
8"
1"
3/4   2 11/16   2 11/16   3/4
1 1/2
1"
2 1/4

4576 - STEP
O.H.S.

1" DRILL   1" DRILL
5/16 DRILL
1" DRILL
3"   9"   9"   3"

4573 - SUPPORT
1 1/4" LORICATED PIPE

CIRCUIT CONTROLLER
110 V.
ACC
1W1   A
B
1GW1
W   G
TRANSFORMER AND CIRCUIT CONTROLLER LOCATED IN STATION
A = 11.0 TO 11.9 VOLTS
B = 22.0 TO 23.0 VOLTS
CONTROL CIRCUITS

PENNSYLVANIA SYSTEM
PRR
STANDARD
SIGNAL
COLOR LIGHT FLAG STATION
STANDARD #S-470-A, FEBRUARY 1929
Redrawn from original PRR drawings
by Jeff Scherb

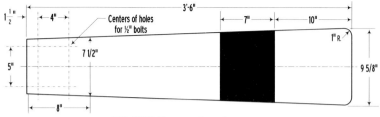

4841 - BLADE. Yellow with Black Stripe
A.R.A. Manual 1924

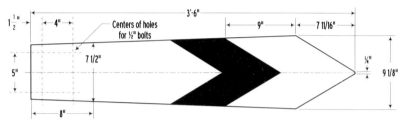

4842 - BLADE. Yellow with Black Stripe
A.R.A. Manual 1924

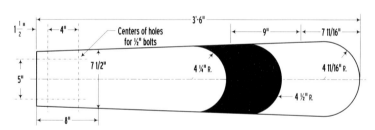

4843 - BLADE. Yellow with Black Stripe

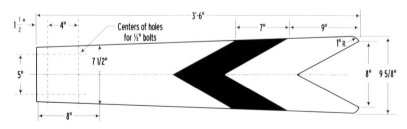

4844 - BLADE. Yellow with Black Stripe

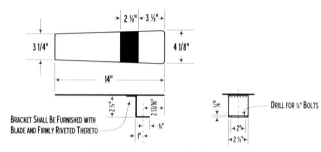

4845 - BLADE. Yellow with Black Stripe

Bracket Shall Be Furnished with Blade and Firmly Riveted Thereto

Drill for ¼" Bolts

NOTE:
1. Blades shall be made of open hearth enameling steel and enameled with not less than three (3) coats of virreous enamel
2. Enamel back of Blades Black
3. Yellow shall be Medium Chrome
4. Unless otherwise specified, Blades shall be furnished with fastenings to fit A.R.A. Standard Semaphore Spectacle.
5. Torque curves and Wind Pressure Test not applicable to Blade 4845

Wind Pressure Test:
Attach the Blade to A.R.A. Standard Semaphore Spectacle; with surfaces of Blade, first toward the front and then the back, parallel and towards the floor, apply a load of 60 pounds to the geometric center of that portion of the Blade extending beyond the fastening. During either of the above tests, the Blade shall not take a permanent set.

PENNSYLVANIA SYSTEM

STANDARD
BLADES
FOR SEMAPHORE SIGNALS

DRAWING #S-484-C, JUNE 1894
REVISED NOV. 1922

Redrawn from original PRR drawings
by Jeff Scherb

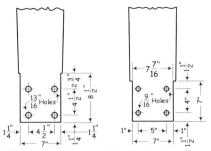

Old Style Semaphore A.A.R. Sig. Sec. Semaphore
FRAMING AND DRILLING OF BOARDS

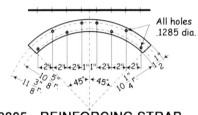

3805 - REINFORCING STRAP
(#14 Galv. Iron)

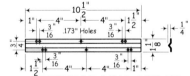

3806 - REINFORCING STRAP
(#16 Annealed Steel)

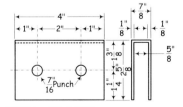

3807 - CLAMP (Sheet Steel)

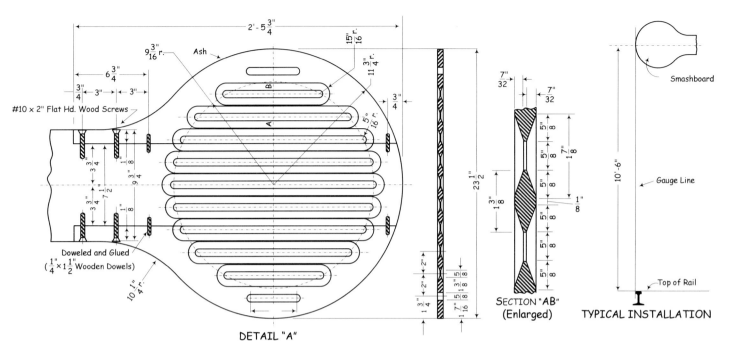

#10 x 2" Flat Hd. Wood Screws

Ash

Doweled and Glued
(1/4" x 1 1/2" Wooden Dowels)

DETAIL "A"

SECTION "AB"
(Enlarged)

Smashboard

Gauge Line

Top of Rail

TYPICAL INSTALLATION

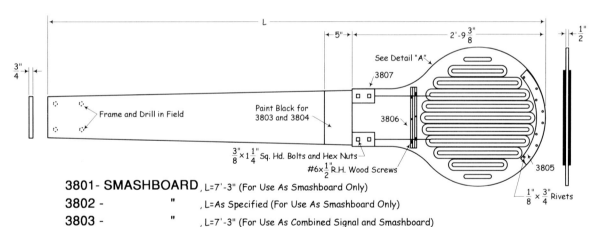

Frame and Drill in Field

See Detail "A"

3807

Paint Black for
3803 and 3804

3806

3/8" x 1 1/4" Sq. Hd. Bolts and Hex Nuts
#6 x 1 1/2" R.H. Wood Screws

3805

1/8" x 3/4" Rivets

3801- SMASHBOARD, L=7'-3" (For Use As Smashboard Only)

3802 -   "   , L=As Specified (For Use As Smashboard Only)

3803 -   "   , L=7'-3" (For Use As Combined Signal and Smashboard)

3804 -   "   , L=As Specified (For Use As Combined Signal and Smashboard)

Paint 3801 and 3802 - Black all over.
Paint 3803 and 3804 - { Front, Medium Chrome Yellow with Black Stripe
                         Back and Edges, Black
When installed as 3803 or 3804, the usual semaphore lamp must be provided
showing Green when board is clear, Red for all other positions.

S-380

THE PENNSLVANIA RAILROAD
STANDARD
SMASHBOARDS
Office of Chief Signal Engineer, Phila., Pa., July 23, 1936
Redrawn from original P.R.R. drawings by Jeff Scherb

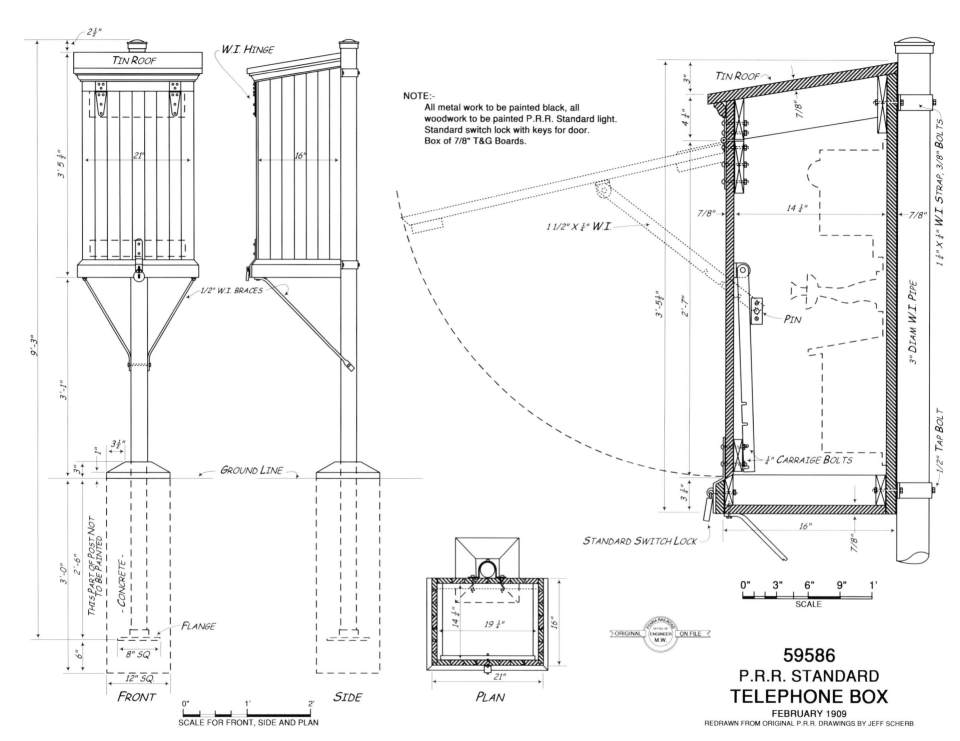

TIN ROOF

W.I. HINGE

2½"

3'-5½"

21"

16"

9'-3"

1/2" W.I. BRACES

3'-1"

3¼"

1"

3"

GROUND LINE

THIS PART OF POST NOT TO BE PAINTED

- CONCRETE -

3'-0"

2'-6"

FLANGE

8" SQ.

6"

12" SQ.

FRONT

SIDE

NOTE:-
All metal work to be painted black, all
woodwork to be painted P.R.R. Standard light.
Standard switch lock with keys for door.
Box of 7/8" T&G Boards.

1 1/2" X ¼" W.I.

PIN

STANDARD SWITCH LOCK

TIN ROOF

3"

4¼"

7/8"

7/8"

14¼"

7/8"

3'-5½"

2'-7"

3"DIAM W.I. PIPE

1¼" X ¼" W.I. STRAP, 3/8" BOLTS

1/2" TAP BOLT

¼" CARRAIGE BOLTS

3¼"

16"

7/8"

PLAN

14¼"

19¼"

16"

21"

0"   3"   6"   9"   1'
SCALE

0"   1'   2'
SCALE FOR FRONT, SIDE AND PLAN

ORIGINAL PENNA RAILROAD OFFICE OF ENGINEER M.W. ON FILE

59586
P.R.R. STANDARD
TELEPHONE BOX
FEBRUARY 1909
REDRAWN FROM ORIGINAL P.R.R. DRAWINGS BY JEFF SCHERB

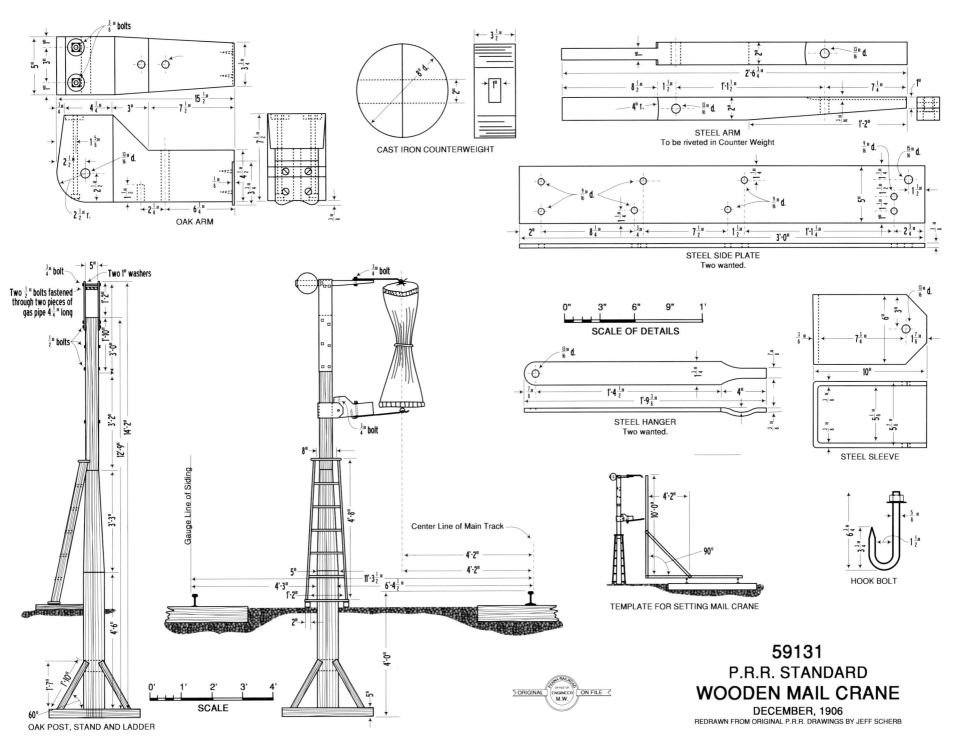

CAST IRON COUNTERWEIGHT

OAK ARM

STEEL ARM
To be riveted in Counter Weight

STEEL SIDE PLATE
Two wanted.

SCALE OF DETAILS
0"   3"   6"   9"   1'

STEEL HANGER
Two wanted.

STEEL SLEEVE

HOOK BOLT

TEMPLATE FOR SETTING MAIL CRANE

OAK POST, STAND AND LADDER

SCALE
0'   1'   2'   3'   4'

Gauge Line of Siding

Center Line of Main Track

Two 1" washers
³⁄₄" bolt

Two ½" bolts fastened
through two pieces of
gas pipe 4¼" long

½" bolts

³⁄₄" bolt

³⁄₄" bolt

59131
P.R.R. STANDARD
WOODEN MAIL CRANE
DECEMBER, 1906
REDRAWN FROM ORIGINAL P.R.R. DRAWINGS BY JEFF SCHERB

PENNA RAILROAD OFFICE OF ENGINEER M.W. — ORIGINAL ON FILE

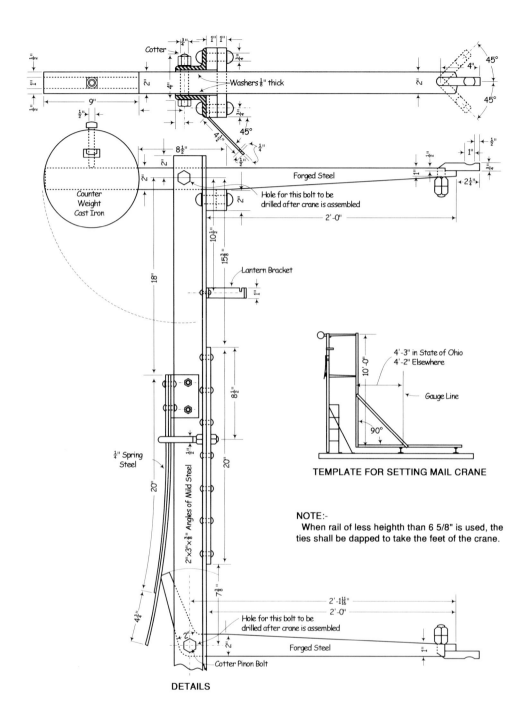

Cotter

Washers ⅛" thick

45°

45°

Forged Steel

Counter Weight Cast Iron

Hole for this bolt to be drilled after crane is assembled

Lantern Bracket

¼" Spring Steel

2"×3"×⅜" Angles of Mild Steel

Hole for this bolt to be drilled after crane is assembled

Forged Steel

Cotter Pinon Bolt

DETAILS

TEMPLATE FOR SETTING MAIL CRANE

4'-3" in State of Ohio
4'-2" Elsewhere

Gauge Line

90°

NOTE:-
When rail of less heighth than 6 5/8" is used, the ties shall be dapped to take the feet of the crane.

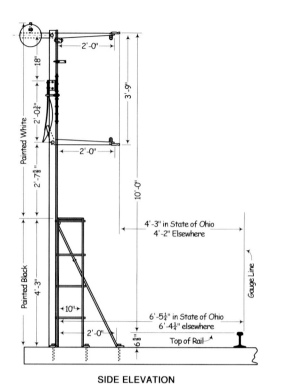

Painted White

Painted Black

4'-3" in State of Ohio
4'-2" Elsewhere

Gauge Line

6'-5¼" in State of Ohio
6'-4¼" elsewhere

Top of Rail

SIDE ELEVATION

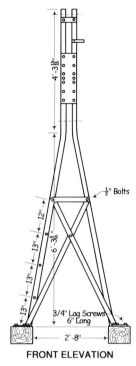

½" Bolts

3/4" Lag Screws 6" Long

FRONT ELEVATION

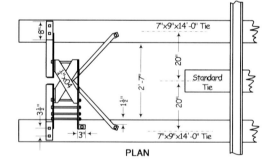

7"×9"×14'-0" Tie

Standard Tie

7"×9"×14'-0" Tie

PLAN

PENNSYLVANIA SYSTEM

STANDARD
MAIL CRANE
STANDARD #70300-A, JANUARY 1922
Redrawn from original PRR drawings
by Jeff Scherb

Signs

P.R.R. Standard Signs

SIGNS, MARKERS AND OTHER INDICATORS were probably the most common items to be found along the right-of-way. The Pennsylvania standards describe a wide variety of signs for all situations, from grade crossings...to stations...to trespassing. Even more numerous perhaps were the mile and section markers, along with signs to identify other aspects of the physical plant, such as bridges.

Unlike the simple painted sheet metal or Scotchlite® signs one might encounter today, many of the signs used a century ago were quite elaborate. Signs of cast iron with raised letters were common, as were custom cast-iron markers for every mile of the right-of-way.

Infrequently modeled, a prototypical collection of signs on the model railroad right-of-way can add great realism and character to the scene.

Most Pennsylvania signs began with the standard Letters and Figures, which today would be called a typeface or perhaps a font. Distinctive and easily recognizable as belonging to the Pennsylvania, the standard letters could be described as a fairly "square" Roman typeface with serifs. Numerals were similar but without the serif. Both normal (p. 66) and condensed (p. 67) versions of these letters and figures were defined by the standard.

Easily recognizable by the keystone shape dominating the center of the sign, passenger station and call signs for interlocking or block stations were unmistakably Pennsylvania. The standard passenger station signs (p. 69) had yellow/gold lettering on a red background, and were made of cast iron with raised letters. These signs would be placed on either end of the station or covered platform, perpendicular to the track.

Station Approach signs (p. 70) were very similar to the station signs, having a central keystone and being made of cast iron. These were placed 200 feet on either side of a passenger station on posts.

The signs were 7' 6" above the ground on these posts.

Passenger stations would typically be adorned with a number of Public Notices (p. 71). These identified the ticket office, restrooms, baggage room, and warnings as necessary, letting passengers know that smoking or spitting was not permitted.

Freight Station Signs (p. 72) are slightly less ornate than passenger station signs, and are generally painted on the side of the structure or on a piece of wood, rather than being cast iron with raised letters. The outline of the sign is also a rounded rectangle and lacks the keystone shape of the passenger sign. The ever-present keystone is present in the painted detail of the sign, however.

Interlocking and Block stations were either given a name similar to a station name or a one- or two-letter designation. The signs for those with full names are similar to passenger station signs, having a keystone outline in the background and being made of cast iron with raised letters (p. 73). Those given a letter designation consist of a cast-iron keystone outline only, with raised letters. Both of these types of signs would be attached to both sides of the interlocking or block station and be placed in a conspicuous location so they could be easily read from a passing train.

Trespass Signs came in a number of different types, depending on the warning necessary. They included simple warnings not to trespass on the railroad or a bridge (p. 74), a more ominous sign warning of penalties for trespassing (p. 75), a sign warning people that a crossing which might be confused for a public crossing was not to be used (p. 76), and one warning of the danger of an electrified third rail, among others. All of these were constructed of cast iron with raised letters; the letters being painted black on a white background.

Whistle and Ring Signs were used to instruct the engineer of the need to sound the whistle or ring the bell. The earlier versions of these were cast-iron posts with a letter "W" or "R" depending on their purpose. The later standard called for a keystone-shaped cast-iron sign with a raised "W" or "R" on a wrought-iron pipe post. Whistle posts were typically placed 1/4 mile from grade crossings and ring signs were placed 160 feet from stations, among other locations.

Mile posts (p. 80) serve as reference points for both operating crews and engineering and maintenance-of-way crews. They record the locations of bridges, signs, structures and other elements of the physical plant. Slow orders and special track conditions were indicated on train orders by mileposts, and a mile number on a maintenance order would indicate the location of maintenance to be performed. Mile measurements commonly started at zero at a major terminal, and branchlines began at zero where they branched from the main. Mile markers were numbered and placed sequentially along the track from the zero reference point. In at least one instance, on the Pennsylvania's Elmira Branch, two mile numbers were skipped when it was discovered that the surveyed mileage used to obtain government approval for construction was found to be two miles short of the minimum required once the roadbed was constructed and the track was laid.

Mile posts were made of cast iron, with raised letters. Similar to mile posts were State and County Line posts, Corporation and Valuation Section posts, and Division posts, all denoting boundaries between their named entities. Mile posts and division posts were located on the engineer's side of the railroad going north and west, and State Line, County Line, Corporation and Valuation Section posts were located on the left side of the railroad going north and west.

Block Limit and Approach Block Limit signs (p. 55) were placed on the engineer's side of the railroad and indicated an upcoming block boundary. As described in the signal chapter, Block Limit and ABL signs were used at unmanned block boundaries on busy lines. The Approach Block Limit sign indicated to the engineer that the train was required to stop ahead, unless a specific Train Order gave permission to pass the block limit without stopping. Typically accompanying a Block Limit sign was a telephone box (p. 60), so the engineer could get permission from the dispatcher to proceed after stopping.

Also out on the right-of-way would be Flanger signs (p. 81). Flangers are small plows or parts of larger plows with blades designed to clean snow from the flangeways of the track. In places were guardrails or other limits to the dimensions inside the rails existed, the flanger would have to raise its blades in order to avoid hitting these obstructions. Flanger signs were typically placed from 50 to 200 feet before grade crossings, switches, bridges, cattle guards and any other place the space between the rails was not clear.

Yard limit signs (pp. 82 and 83) were used to delineate boundaries between road and yard territory. These would be placed on the engineer's side of track, facing incoming trains. Slow signs (p. 83) were placed at locations where slow operation was the rule, such as congested industrial trackage, and areas with particularly dangerous or numerous grade crossings.

Also at grade crossings, but facing oncoming motorists rather than trains, were Road Crossing signs (pp. 84-88). Various styles of these were used over the years, and usage also depended on the importance or risk of the crossing. At a lightly trafficked country road crossing, a simple "Look Out for the Locomotive" sign might have been used, in either an oval shape (p. 84) or on a crossbuck (p. 87). Some early crossing signs in towns were placed in the center of the road on concrete foundations painted in a checkerboard pattern (p. 88). Particularly risky crossings in highly trafficked areas might have used illuminated stop signs (p. 85) in addition to other static warning signs. By the middle of the last century, almost all crossing signs were replaced with the A.A.R. standard sign (p. 86), consisting of "Railroad Crossing" crossbucks over alternately flashing lights.

In most locations, Road approach signs (p. 89) were also placed 200 feet up the road from the grade crossing to warn motorists of the crossing ahead. Different states had slightly different regulations for the placement of these signs, and Virginia law specified a different sign altogether. ▼

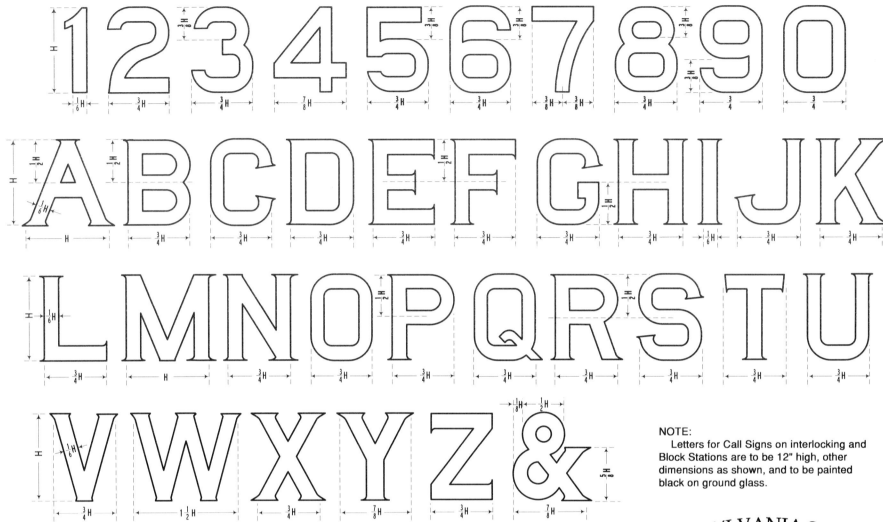

NOTE:
Letters for Call Signs on interlocking and Block Stations are to be 12" high, other dimensions as shown, and to be painted black on ground glass.

PENNSYLVANIA SYSTEM

60146

STANDARD
LETTERS AND FIGURES
FOR
SIGNS AND NOTICES
JULY 1920

Redrawn from original PRR drawings by Jeff Scherb

When necessary to use a condensed form of the letter, the horizontal dimensions, except the thickness of the body of the letter, shall be two-thirds of that shown above, thus>

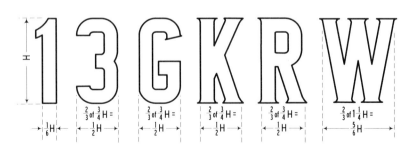

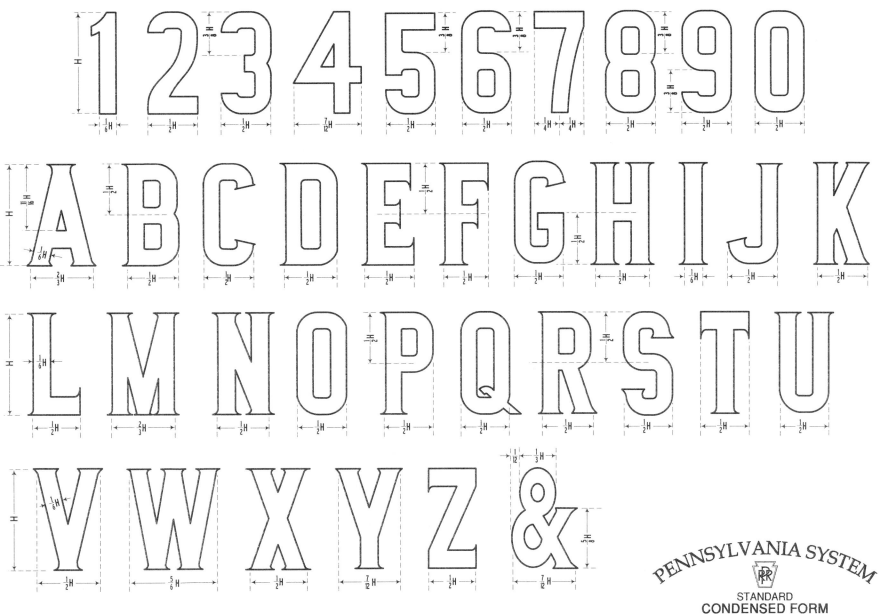

NOTE:
Letters for Call Signs on interlocking and Block Stations are to be 12" high, other dimensions as shown, and to be painted black on ground glass.

PENNSYLVANIA SYSTEM
STANDARD
CONDENSED FORM
LETTERS AND FIGURES
FOR
SIGNS AND NOTICES
Drawn to PRR specifications by Jeff Scherb

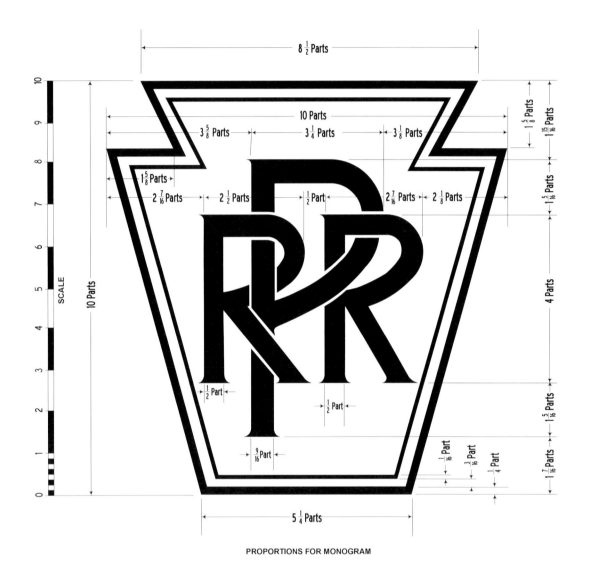

SCALE

8 ½ Parts

10 Parts

3 ⅝ Parts   3 ¼ Parts   3 ⅛ Parts

1 ⅝ Parts

1 ⁵⁄₁₆ Parts

10 Parts

1 ⅝ Parts

2 ⁷⁄₁₆ Parts   2 ½ Parts   ½ Part   2 ⁷⁄₁₆ Parts   2 ⅛ Parts

1 ⅝ Parts

1 ⁵⁄₁₆ Parts

4 Parts

½ Part   ½ Part

1 ⅝ Parts

1 ⁵⁄₁₆ Parts

⁹⁄₁₆ Part

1⁄₁₆ Part   3⁄₁₆ Part   ¼ Part

1 ⁷⁄₁₆ Parts

1 ⁷⁄₁₆ Parts

5 ¼ Parts

PROPORTIONS FOR MONOGRAM

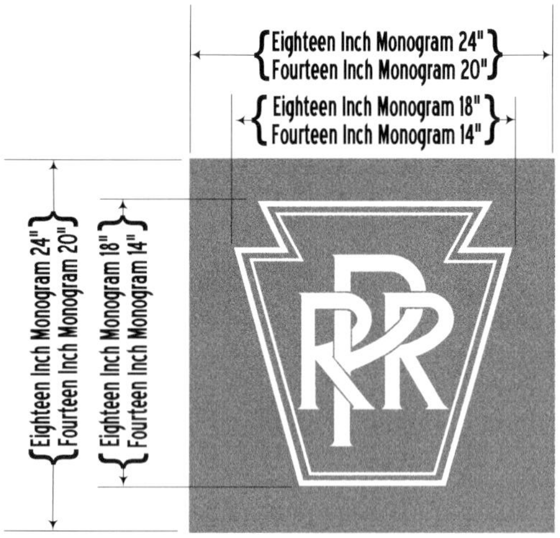

{ Eighteen Inch Monogram 24" }
{ Fourteen Inch Monogram 20" }

{ Eighteen Inch Monogram 18" }
{ Fourteen Inch Monogram 14" }

{ Eighteen Inch Monogram 24" }
{ Fourteen Inch Monogram 20" }

{ Eighteen Inch Monogram 18" }
{ Fourteen Inch Monogram 14" }

STENCILS

NOTE:

In large reproductions, excepting the markings on bridges, the body of the letters shall be gold, the outline and fine innerline of the keystone and the outline of the letters shall be black and the ground tuscan red.

In small press or embossed work the body of the letters and the outline and fine innerline of the keystone shall be gold or black, or the ground may be made of tuscan red leaving the letters and fine innerline of the keystone the color of the surface on which it is reproduced.

In preparation of the various brands and dies necessary for branding wood or stamping metal the fine innerline shall be omitted from the design.

Stencils for Bridges shall be made of #30 (Browne and Sharpe Gauge) copper. The ties required to unite the parts of the design may be made of the sizes and in the position as determined by the general practice of the makers.

The Stencils are for use in painting the monogram on girder, I beam and reinforced concrete slab bridges, spanning streets and highways.

The monogram shall be painted on both outside surfaces of the bridge over the centerline of the street or highway, where it is in a plain space without interruption by angles. Where it cannot be placed over the centerline of the street or highway it shall be located in the second full sized panel from the righthand end of the bridge, facing it.

The Eighteen inch Monogram shall be used in marking girder bridges and the Fourteen inch for marking other structures.

On bridges painted black or dark color the monogram shall be painted white. On bridges painted light color (required in some cities) the monogram shall be painted black.

78150

PENNSYLVANIA SYSTEM

STANDARD
MONOGRAM
AND
STENCILS FOR MARKING BRIDGES
1921

Redrawn from original PRR drawings by Jeff Scherb

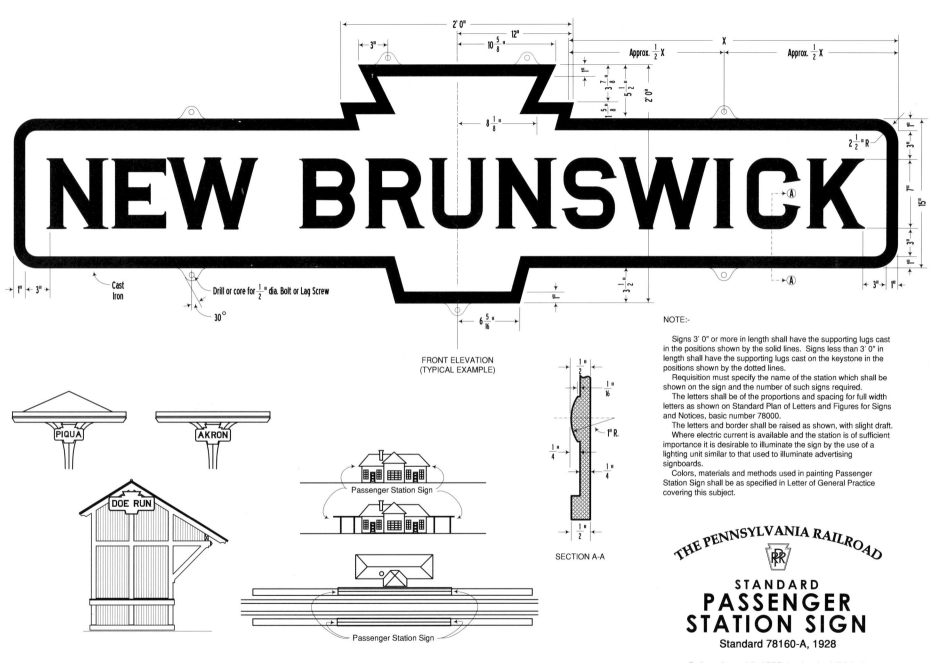

NEW BRUNSWICK

Cast Iron

Drill or core for ½" dia. Bolt or Lag Screw

30°

FRONT ELEVATION
(TYPICAL EXAMPLE)

PIQUA

AKRON

DOE RUN

Passenger Station Sign

Passenger Station Sign

SKETCHES SHOWING LOCATIONS OF SIGNS

SECTION A-A

NOTE:-

Signs 3' 0" or more in length shall have the supporting lugs cast in the positions shown by the solid lines. Signs less than 3' 0" in length shall have the supporting lugs cast on the keystone in the positions shown by the dotted lines.

Requisition must specify the name of the station which shall be shown on the sign and the number of such signs required.

The letters shall be of the proportions and spacing for full width letters as shown on Standard Plan of Letters and Figures for Signs and Notices, basic number 78000.

The letters and border shall be raised as shown, with slight draft.

Where electric current is available and the station is of sufficient importance it is desirable to illuminate the sign by the use of a lighting unit similar to that used to illuminate advertising signboards.

Colors, materials and methods used in painting Passenger Station Sign shall be as specified in Letter of General Practice covering this subject.

THE PENNSYLVANIA RAILROAD

PRR

STANDARD
PASSENGER
STATION SIGN

Standard 78160-A, 1928

Redrawn from original PRR drawings by Jeff Scherb

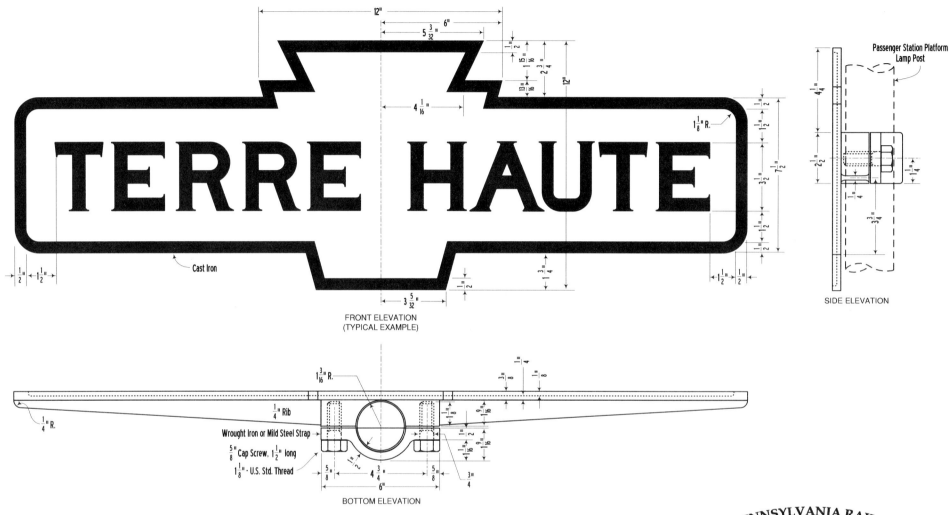

FRONT ELEVATION
(TYPICAL EXAMPLE)

SIDE ELEVATION

BOTTOM ELEVATION

NOTE:

Requisition must specify the name of the station which shall be shown on the sign and the number of such signs required.

The letters shall be of the proportions and spacing for full width letters as shown on Standard Plan of Letters and Figures for Signs and Notices, basic number 78000.

At unimportant stations where there is a Passenger Station Sign the Passenger Station Approach Sign may be omitted

The signs shall be attached to the Station Platform Lamp Posts which are situated about 200 feet on either side of the passenger station, and at a height on the posts of 7 feet 6 inches, measured from the bottom of the sign to the top of the platform.

Colors, materials and methods used in painting Passenger Station Sign shall be as specified in Letter of General Practice covering this subject.

The letters and border shall be raised 1/4 inch, with slight draft.

THE PENNSYLVANIA RAILROAD

STANDARD
PASSENGER
STATION
APPROACH SIGN

Standard 78161-A, 1928

Redrawn from original PRR drawings by Jeff Scherb

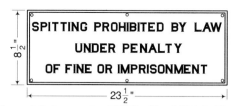

Shown full size on plan 59771. Sheet Metal. Mars Red Medium Background. Gold Letters outlined with Black. Gold Yellow Border.

Shown full size on plan 5997. Sheet Metal. White Background. Black Letters and Border.

Shown full size on plan 60009. Sheet Metal. Mars Red Medium Background. Gold Letters outlined with Black. Gold Yellow Border.

Shown full size on plan 60401. Sheet Metal. Mars Red Medium Background. Gold Letters outlined with Black. Gold Yellow Border.

Shown full size on plan 60400. Sheet Metal. Mars Red Medium Background. Gold Letters outlined with Black. Gold Yellow Border.

Shown full size on plan 60399. Sheet Metal. Mars Red Medium Background. Gold Letters outlined with Black. Gold Yellow Border.

Shown full size on plan 60396. Sheet Metal. Mars Red Medium Background. Gold Letters outlined with Black. Gold Yellow Border.

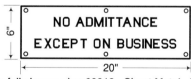

Shown full size on plan 60019. Sheet Metal. Mars Red Medium Background. Gold Letters outlined with Black. Gold Yellow Border.

Shown full size on plan 60398. Sheet Metal. Mars Red Medium Background. Gold Letters outlined with Black. Gold Yellow Border.

Shown full size on plan 60402. Sheet Metal. Mars Red Medium Background. Gold Letters outlined with Black. Gold Yellow Border.

Shown full size on plan 60397. Sheet Metal. Mars Red Medium Background. Gold Letters outlined with Black. Gold Yellow Border.

Shown full size, with method of attaching, on plan 60116. Sheet Metal. Mars Red Medium Background. Gold Letters outlined with Black. Gold Yellow Border.

NOTE:-
    Where it is not possible to attach the metal sign these notices may be painted directly upon the wall

SCALE

59387
P.R.R. STANDARD
PUBLIC NOTICES
SEPTEMBER 1909
REDRAWN FROM ORIGINAL P.R.R. DRAWINGS BY JEFF SCHERB

FRONT ELEVATION OF SIGN FOR FREIGHT STATION WHERE IT IS DESIRABLE TO DISPLAY THE SPECIFIC NAME
(TYPICAL EXAMPLE)

FRONT ELEVATION OF SIGN FOR FREIGHT STATION WHERE IT IS NOT NECESSARY TO DISPLAY THE SPECIFIC NAME
(TYPICAL EXAMPLE)

NOTE:

The sign may be either painted on the building, or made of wood or other suitable material and fastened securely to the building in a conspicuous position.

The letters in the words "The Pennsylvania Railroad" shall be of the proportions and spacing for condensed letters and in all other words the forms shall be of the full width forms, as shown on Standard Plan of Letters and Figures for Signs and Notices, basic number 78000.

The monograms shall be proportioned in accordance with the Standard Plan of Monogram, basic number 78150.

Colors, materials and methods used in painting Freight Station Signs shall be as specified in Letter of General Practice covering this subject.

PENNSYLVANIA SYSTEM

FREIGHT STATION
SIGNS

STANDARD #78165-A

Redrawn from original PRR drawings by Jeff Scherb

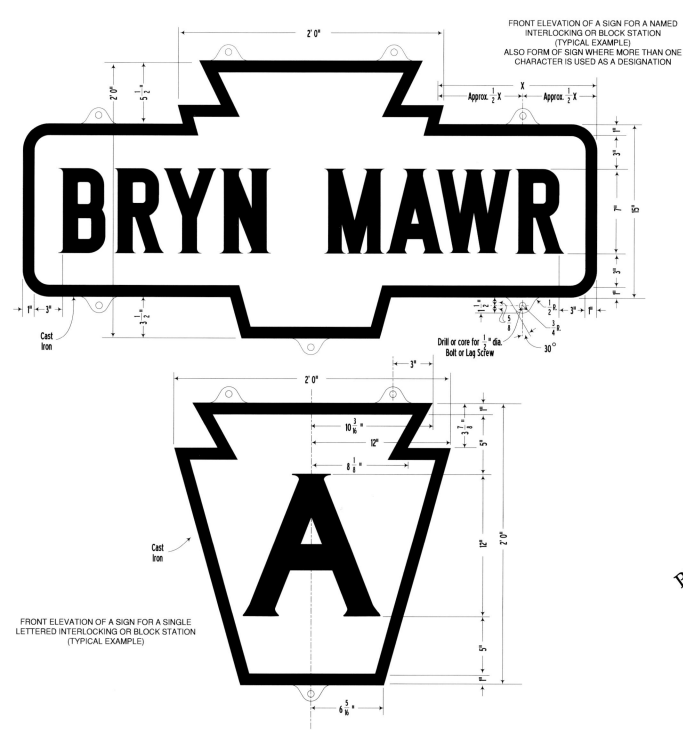

FRONT ELEVATION OF A SIGN FOR A NAMED
INTERLOCKING OR BLOCK STATION
(TYPICAL EXAMPLE)
ALSO FORM OF SIGN WHERE MORE THAN ONE
CHARACTER IS USED AS A DESIGNATION

Cast
Iron

Drill or core for $\frac{1}{2}$" dia.
Bolt or Lag Screw

FRONT ELEVATION OF A SIGN FOR A SINGLE
LETTERED INTERLOCKING OR BLOCK STATION
(TYPICAL EXAMPLE)

Cast
Iron

NOTE:

Signs 3' 0" or more in length shall have the supporting lugs cast in the positions as shown by the solid lines. Signs less than 3' 0" in length shall have the supporting lugs cast on the keystone in the positions shown by the dotted lines.

Requisition must specify the name, character or characters designating the call of the Interlocking or Block station which shall be shown on the sign and the number of such signs required.

On Interlocking or Block stations designated by name the letters shall be of the proportions and spacing for the condensed letters as shown on Standard Plan of Letters and Figures for Signs and Notices, basic number 78000 and where designated by letters or numbers, figure or figures, or both, they shall be of the proportions and spacing for the full width forms shown on said Standard Plan.

The characters and border shall be raised 1/8 inch, with slight draft.

Two signs shall be attached to each Interlocking or Block station, placed in conspicuous positions, one on each side of the building so that they may be easily read from approaching or receding trains.

When attaching the sign to a flat surface, furring strips shall be used to hold the sign away from the surface about 1 inch.

Before leaving the foundry, the manufacturer shall thoroughly clean all surfaces of the casting and apply a priming coat of Red Lead (M.P. Specification No. 155)

Colors, materials and methods used in painting Call Signs for Interlocking or Block Stations shall be as specified in instructions for Painting Structural Street, Building and Station Signs.

PENNSYLVANIA SYSTEM

STANDARD
CALL SIGNS
FOR
**INTERLOCKING OR
BLOCK STATIONS**

STANDARD #78163-B, 1928
Redrawn from original PRR drawings
by Jeff Scherb

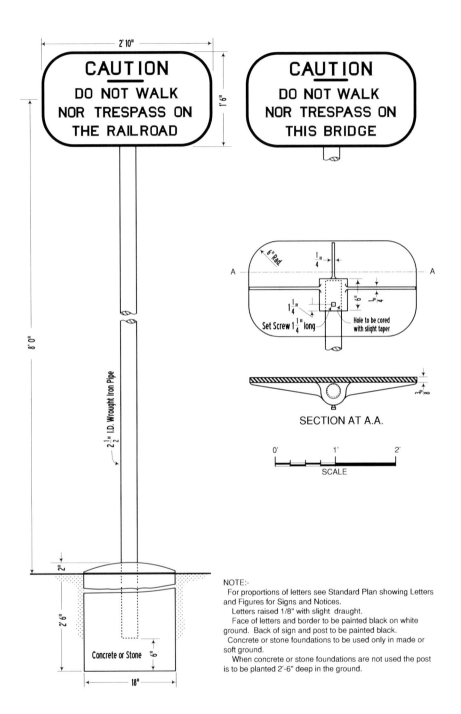

CAUTION

DO NOT WALK
NOR TRESPASS ON
THE RAILROAD

2' 10"

1' 6"

CAUTION

DO NOT WALK
NOR TRESPASS ON
THIS BRIDGE

8' 0"

2½" I.D. Wrought Iron Pipe

2' 6"

2"

6"

Concrete or Stone

18"

6" Rad.

¼"

¼"

1¼"

6"

Set Screw 1¼" long

Hole to be cored
with slight taper

A — A

SECTION AT A.A.

3/8"

0'   1'   2'

SCALE

NOTE:-
   For proportions of letters see Standard Plan showing Letters
and Figures for Signs and Notices.
   Letters raised 1/8" with slight draught.
   Face of letters and border to be painted black on white
ground. Back of sign and post to be painted black.
   Concrete or stone foundations to be used only in made or
soft ground.
   When concrete or stone foundations are not used the post
is to be planted 2'-6" deep in the ground.

¾"

1¼"

2½"

2½"

2"

1½"

8 3/16"

10 3/16"

3/8"

3 11/16"

Centre Line of Sign

0"   1"   2"   3"

SCALE

THE PENNSYLVANIA RAILROAD

P R R

STANDARD
TRESPASS SIGN

STANDARD #61821-D, JUNE 1898, REVISED DEC. 1914

Redrawn from original PRR drawings by Jeff Scherb

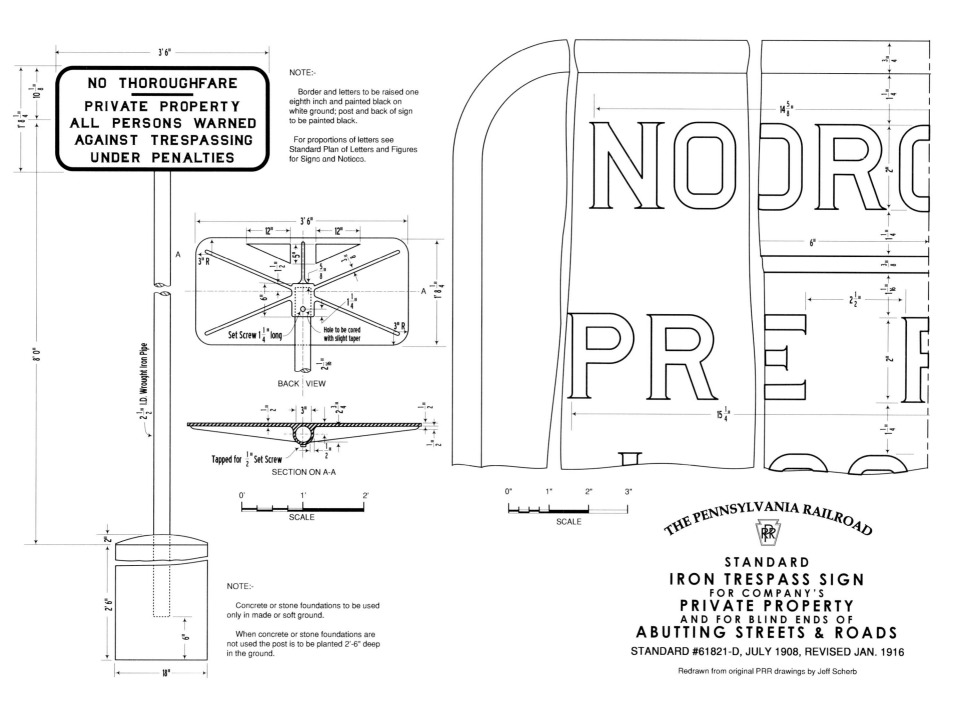

NO THOROUGHFARE

PRIVATE PROPERTY
ALL PERSONS WARNED
AGAINST TRESPASSING
UNDER PENALTIES

3' 6"

10 1/8"

1' 8 3/4"

8' 0"

2 1/2" I.D. Wrought Iron Pipe

A

2"

2' 6"

6"

18"

NOTE:-

Border and letters to be raised one eighth inch and painted black on white ground; post and back of sign to be painted black.

For proportions of letters see Standard Plan of Letters and Figures for Signs and Notices.

BACK VIEW

3' 6"
12"   12"
3" R
5"
1/2
5/8
3/8
6"
1 1/4"
Set Screw 1 1/4" long
Hole to be cored with slight taper
3" R
1' 8 3/4"
A
2 1/16"

SECTION ON A-A

3"
1/2
2 3/4"
1/2
1/2
1/2
Tapped for 1/2" Set Screw

0'   1'   2'
SCALE

NOTE:-

Concrete or stone foundations to be used only in made or soft ground.

When concrete or stone foundations are not used the post is to be planted 2'-6" deep in the ground.

NO DR...
PR E...

14 5/8"
3/4
1/4
6"
3/8
1/16
2 1/2
2"
15 1/4"
1/4

0"   1"   2"   3"
SCALE

THE PENNSYLVANIA RAILROAD

STANDARD
IRON TRESPASS SIGN
FOR COMPANY'S
PRIVATE PROPERTY
AND FOR BLIND ENDS OF
ABUTTING STREETS & ROADS
STANDARD #61821-D, JULY 1908, REVISED JAN. 1916

Redrawn from original PRR drawings by Jeff Scherb

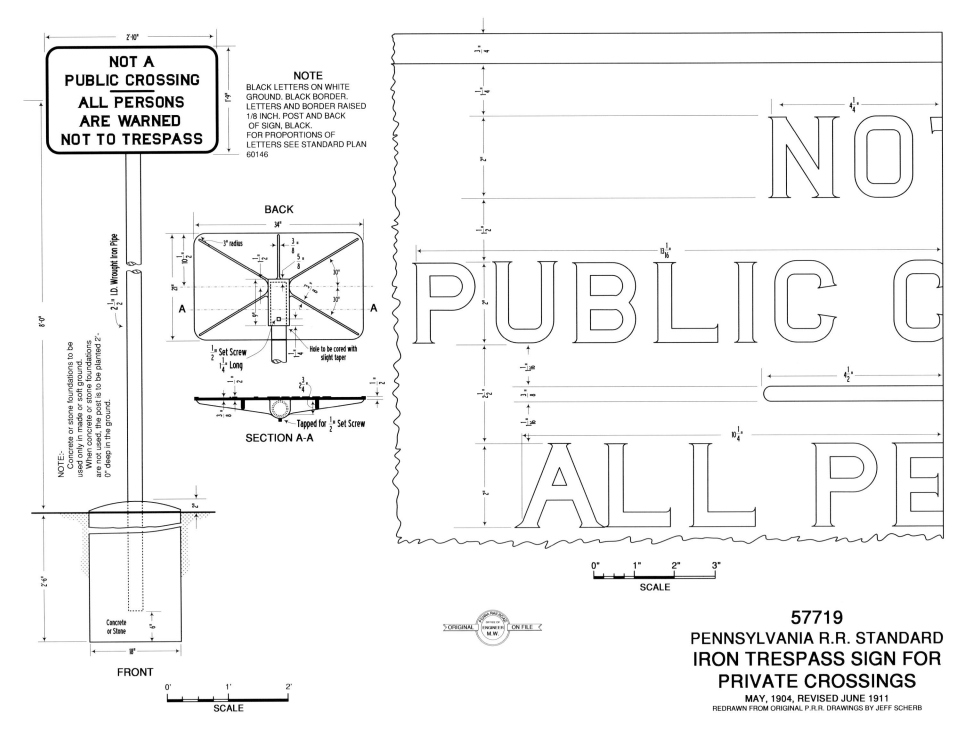

NOT A PUBLIC CROSSING

ALL PERSONS ARE WARNED NOT TO TRESPASS

2'-10"

1'-9"

NOTE
BLACK LETTERS ON WHITE GROUND. BLACK BORDER. LETTERS AND BORDER RAISED 1/8 INCH. POST AND BACK OF SIGN, BLACK. FOR PROPORTIONS OF LETTERS SEE STANDARD PLAN 60146

2½" I.D. Wrought Iron Pipe

8'-0"

NOTE:- Concrete or stone foundations to be used only in made or soft ground. When concrete or stone foundations are not used, the post is to be planted 2'-0" deep in the ground.

BACK

34"

10½"

3" radius

3/8"
5/8"

21"

30°
30°

½" Set Screw 1¼" Long

9"

Hole to be cored with slight taper

A ———— A

SECTION A-A

2¾"

3/8"

Tapped for ½" Set Screw

2"

2'-6"

6"

Concrete or Stone

18"

FRONT

0'   1'   2'
SCALE

3/4"

1/4"

2"

1/2"

13 1/16"

2"

1 1/16"

2 1/2"

3/8"

1 1/16"

2"

4 1/4"

4 1/2"

10 1/4"

NO

PUBLIC C

ALL PE

0"   1"   2"   3"
SCALE

PENNA RAILROAD
OFFICE OF
ENGINEER
M.W.
◁ ORIGINAL   ON FILE ▷

57719
PENNSYLVANIA R.R. STANDARD
IRON TRESPASS SIGN FOR
PRIVATE CROSSINGS
MAY, 1904, REVISED JUNE 1911
REDRAWN FROM ORIGINAL P.R.R. DRAWINGS BY JEFF SCHERB

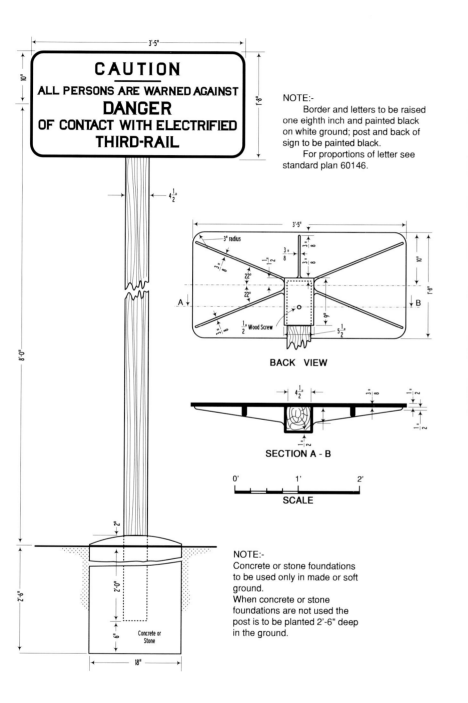

CAUTION

ALL PERSONS ARE WARNED AGAINST

DANGER

OF CONTACT WITH ELECTRIFIED

THIRD-RAIL

NOTE:-
Border and letters to be raised one eighth inch and painted black on white ground; post and back of sign to be painted black.
For proportions of letter see standard plan 60146.

BACK VIEW

SECTION A - B

SCALE

NOTE:-
Concrete or stone foundations to be used only in made or soft ground.
When concrete or stone foundations are not used the post is to be planted 2'-6" deep in the ground.

Concrete or Stone

SCALE

ORIGINAL ON FILE

58969
P.R.R. STANDARD
IRON WARNING SIGN
FOR ELECTRIFIED TRACKS
JULY, 1906
REDRAWN FROM ORIGINAL P.R.R. DRAWINGS BY JEFF SCHERB

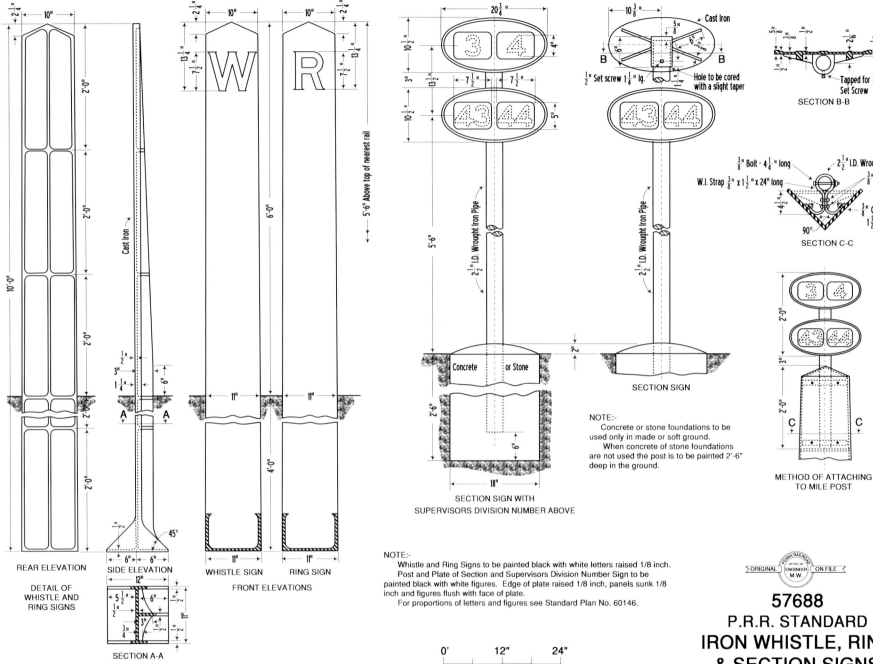

REAR ELEVATION

DETAIL OF WHISTLE AND RING SIGNS

SIDE ELEVATION

SECTION A-A

WHISTLE SIGN

RING SIGN

FRONT ELEVATIONS

Cast Iron

5'-6" Above top of nearest rail

2½" I.D. Wrought Iron Pipe

Concrete   or Stone

SECTION SIGN WITH SUPERVISORS DIVISION NUMBER ABOVE

2½" I.D. Wrought Iron Pipe

SECTION SIGN

NOTE:-
Concrete or stone foundations to be used only in made or soft ground.
When concrete of stone foundations are not used the post is to be painted 2'-6" deep in the ground.

Cast Iron

½" Set screw 1¼" lg.   Hole to be cored with a slight taper

SECTION B-B

Tapped for ½" Set Screw

⅜" Bolt · 4¼" long   2½" I.D. Wrought Iron Pipe
W.I. Strap ⅜" x 1½" x 24" long   ⅜" Rivets
⅜" Countersunk Bolt 1½" Long
90°

SECTION C-C

METHOD OF ATTACHING TO MILE POST

NOTE:-
Whistle and Ring Signs to be painted black with white letters raised 1/8 inch.
Post and Plate of Section and Supervisors Division Number Sign to be painted black with white figures. Edge of plate raised 1/8 inch, panels sunk 1/8 inch and figures flush with face of plate.
For proportions of letters and figures see Standard Plan No. 60146.

0'   12"   24"

SCALE

ORIGINAL ENGINEER ON FILE
PENNA RAILROAD OFFICE OF M.W.

57688
P.R.R. STANDARD
IRON WHISTLE, RING
& SECTION SIGNS
MAY 1905
REDRAWN FROM ORIGINAL P.R.R. DRAWINGS BY JEFF SCHERB

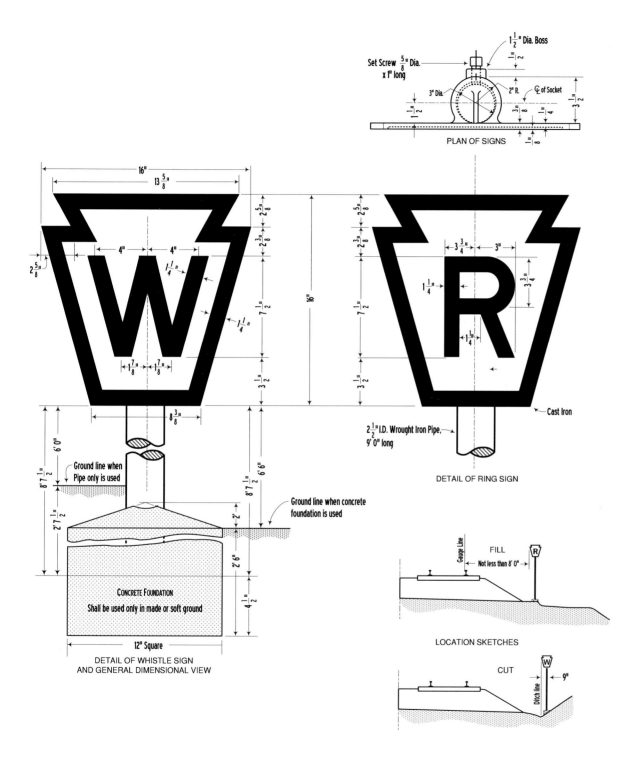

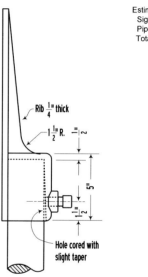

NOTE:

Letters and borders shall be raised ___ inch with slight draft.

All parts of sign shall be painted black except the background which shall be white.

Except where regulated by local ordinances or other laws the prescribed sign shall be located at a distance of less than 1200 feet nor more than 1650 feet in advance of the grade road crossing or point for which the warning is to be sounded.

Whistle and Ring signs of earlier design shall have the face and edges painted white from a distance of 18 inches above the ground line upward, the letter and all other parts black.

PLAN OF SIGNS

Estimated Weight
Sign: 23 ¼ lbs.
Pipe: 52 ¼ lbs.
Total: 75 ½ lbs.

DETAIL OF RING SIGN

2½" I.D. Wrought Iron Pipe, 9' 0" long

Cast Iron

SIDE ELEVATION OF SIGNS

Rib ¼" thick
1½" R.
Hole cored with slight taper

Ground line when Pipe only is used

Ground line when concrete foundation is used

CONCRETE FOUNDATION
Shall be used only in made or soft ground

12" Square

DETAIL OF WHISTLE SIGN AND GENERAL DIMENSIONAL VIEW

FILL
Not less than 8' 0"
Gauge Line

LOCATION SKETCHES

CUT
Ditch line
9"

THE PENNSYLVANIA RAILROAD

PRR

STANDARD
WHISTLE AND RING SIGNS
Standard 78408-B 1929

Redrawn from original PRR drawings by Jeff Scherb

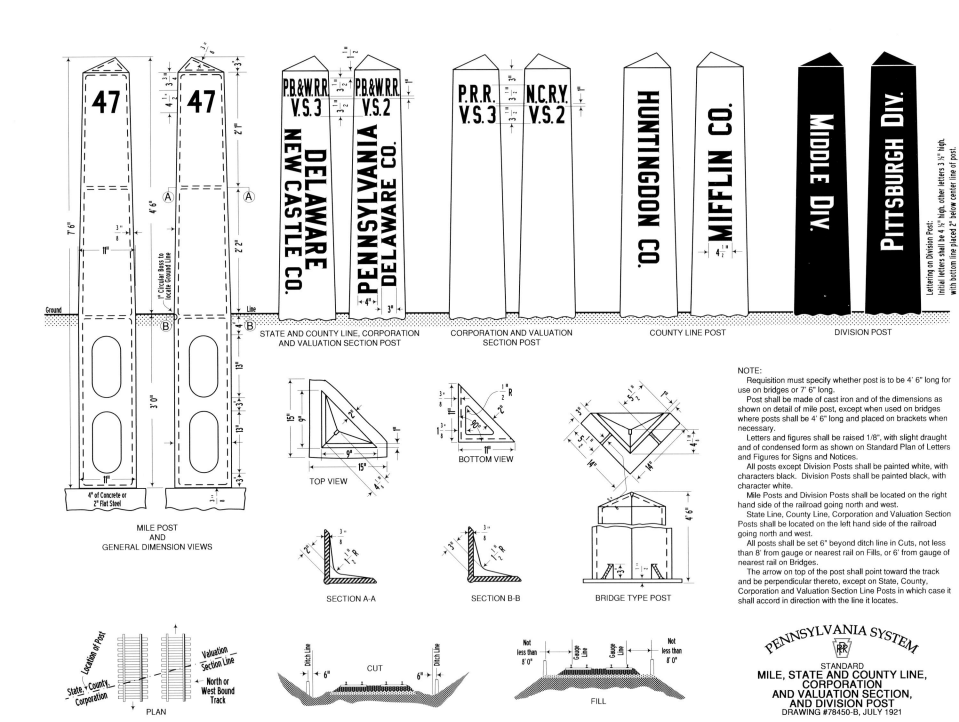

NOTE:
Requisition must specify whether post is to be 4' 6" long for use on bridges or 7' 6" long.

Post shall be made of cast iron and of the dimensions as shown on detail of mile post, except when used on bridges where posts shall be 4' 6" long and placed on brackets when necessary.

Letters and figures shall be raised 1/8", with slight draught and of condensed form as shown on Standard Plan of Letters and Figures for Signs and Notices.

All posts except Division Posts shall be painted white, with characters black. Division Posts shall be painted black, with character white.

Mile Posts and Division Posts shall be located on the right hand side of the railroad going north and west.

State Line, County Line, Corporation and Valuation Section Posts shall be located on the left hand side of the railroad going north and west.

All posts shall be set 6" beyond ditch line in Cuts, not less than 8' from gauge or nearest rail on Fills, or 6' from gauge of nearest rail on Bridges.

The arrow on top of the post shall point toward the track and be perpendicular thereto, except on State, County, Corporation and Valuation Section Line Posts in which case it shall accord in direction with the line it locates.

PENNSYLVANIA SYSTEM

STANDARD
MILE, STATE AND COUNTY LINE,
CORPORATION
AND VALUATION SECTION,
AND DIVISION POST
DRAWING #78450-B, JULY 1921

Redrawn from original PRR drawings by Jeff Scherb

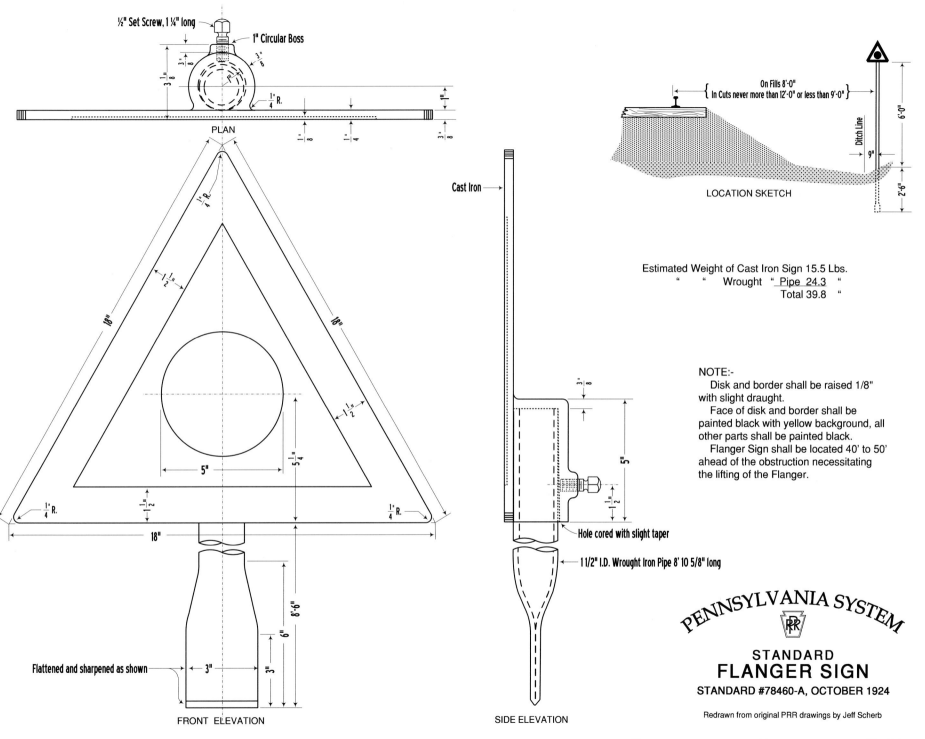

½" Set Screw, 1 ¼" long

1" Circular Boss

PLAN

1" R.
¼

⅜"
⅛"
¼"
⅜"

3 ⅛"
⅜"

On Fills 8'-0"
In Cuts never more than 12'-0" or less than 9'-0"

Ditch Line

6'-0"

9"

2'-6"

LOCATION SKETCH

Cast Iron →

1" R.
¼

18"

18"

1 ½"

1 ½"

5"

5 ¼"

1 ½"

1" R.
¼

1" R.
¼

18"

Estimated Weight of Cast Iron Sign 15.5 Lbs.
"   "   Wrought " Pipe 24.3 "
Total 39.8 "

NOTE:-
   Disk and border shall be raised 1/8"
with slight draught.
   Face of disk and border shall be
painted black with yellow background, all
other parts shall be painted black.
   Flanger Sign shall be located 40' to 50'
ahead of the obstruction necessitating
the lifting of the Flanger.

⅜"

5"

1 ½"

Hole cored with slight taper

8'-6"

6"

3"

3"

Flattened and sharpened as shown

3"

FRONT ELEVATION

← 1 1/2" I.D. Wrought Iron Pipe 8' 10 5/8" long

SIDE ELEVATION

PENNSYLVANIA SYSTEM

PRR

STANDARD
FLANGER SIGN
STANDARD #78460-A, OCTOBER 1924

Redrawn from original PRR drawings by Jeff Scherb

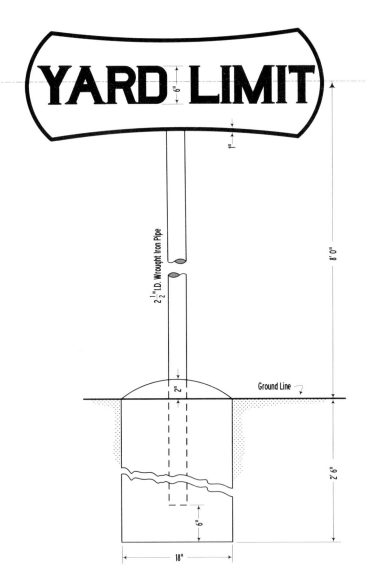

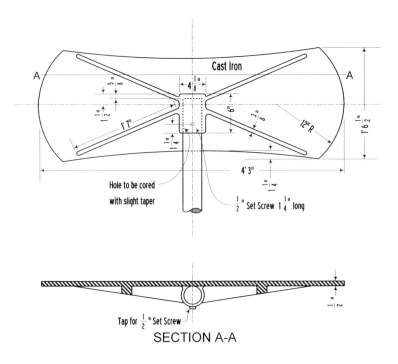

SECTION A-A

NOTE:
    Concrete or stone foundations shall be used only in made or soft ground.
    When cocrete or stone foundations are not used the post is to be planted 2' 6" deep in the ground.
    Face of letters and border of sign shall be painted black with white ground, back of sign and post painted black.
    Letters and borders shall be raised 1/8 inch with slight draft.
    For proportions of letters see Standard Plan showing Letters and Figures for Signs and Notices.

PENNSYLVANIA SYSTEM

STANDARD
YARD LIMIT SIGN

STANDARD #78400-A, 1920

Redrawn from original PRR drawings by Jeff Scherb

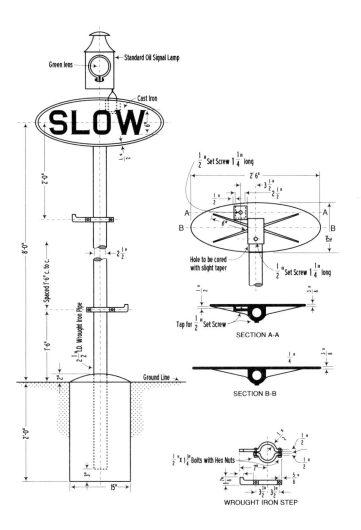

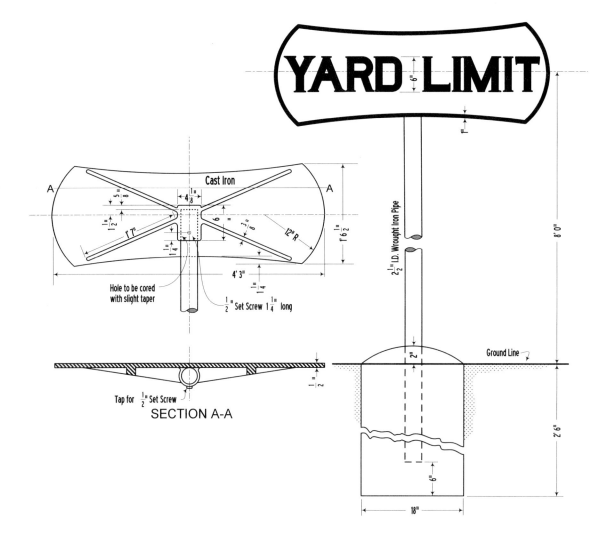

NOTE:

Concrete or stone foundations shall be used only in made or soft ground.

When cocrete or stone foundations are not used the post is to be planted 2' 6" deep in the ground.

Face of letters and border of Slow sign shall be painted white with green ground.

Face of letters and border of Yard Limit sign shall be painted black with white ground.

Back of sign and post to be painted black.

Letters and borders shall be raised 1/8 inch with slight draft.

For proportions of letters see Standard Plan 60146.

59390
P.R.R. STANDARD
SLOW & YARD LIMIT SIGNS
OCTOBER, 1912
REDRAWN FROM ORIGINAL P.R.R. DRAWINGS BY JEFF SCHERB

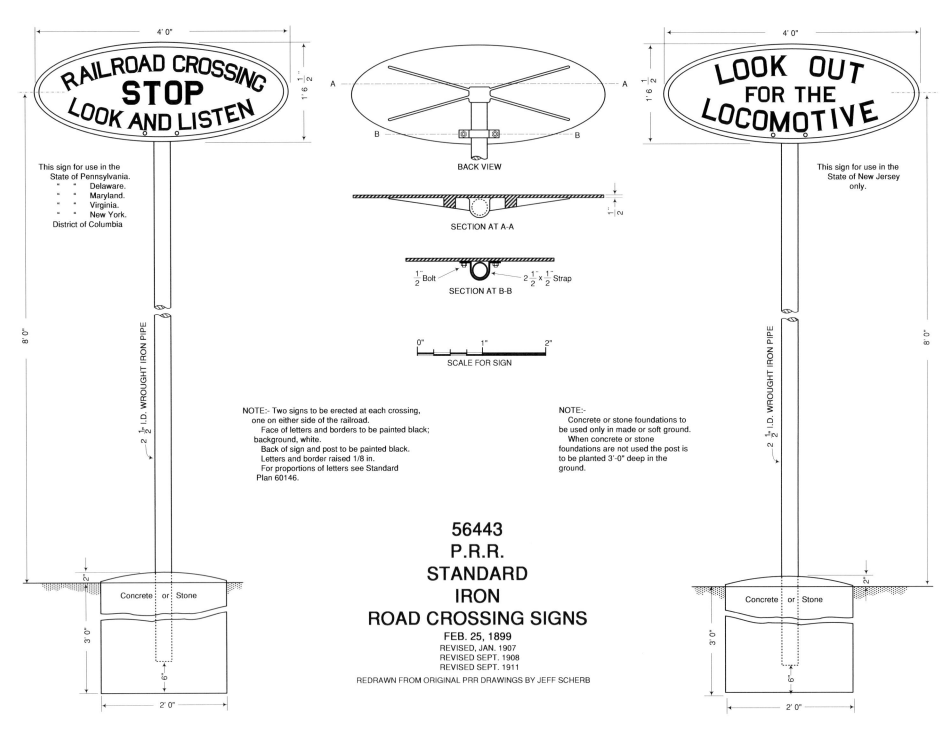

RAILROAD CROSSING
STOP
LOOK AND LISTEN

4' 0"

1' 6 1/2"

This sign for use in the
State of Pennsylvania.
"   "   Delaware.
"   "   Maryland.
"   "   Virginia.
"   "   New York.
District of Columbia

8' 0"

2 1/2" I.D. WROUGHT IRON PIPE

Concrete   or   Stone

2"

3' 0"

6"

2' 0"

BACK VIEW

A —————————— A

B —————————— B

SECTION AT A-A

1/2"

1/2" Bolt   2 1/2" x 1/2" Strap

SECTION AT B-B

0"   1"   2"

SCALE FOR SIGN

NOTE:- Two signs to be erected at each crossing,
   one on either side of the railroad.
      Face of letters and borders to be painted black;
background, white.
      Back of sign and post to be painted black.
      Letters and border raised 1/8 in.
      For proportions of letters see Standard
Plan 60146.

NOTE:-
      Concrete or stone foundations to
be used only in made or soft ground.
      When concrete or stone
foundations are not used the post is
to be planted 3'-0" deep in the
ground.

56443
P.R.R.
STANDARD
IRON
ROAD CROSSING SIGNS
FEB. 25, 1899
REVISED, JAN. 1907
REVISED SEPT. 1908
REVISED SEPT. 1911
REDRAWN FROM ORIGINAL PRR DRAWINGS BY JEFF SCHERB

LOOK OUT
FOR THE
LOCOMOTIVE

4' 0"

1' 6 1/2"

This sign for use in the
State of New Jersey
only.

8' 0"

2 1/2" I.D. WROUGHT IRON PIPE

Concrete   or   Stone

2"

3' 0"

6"

2' 0"

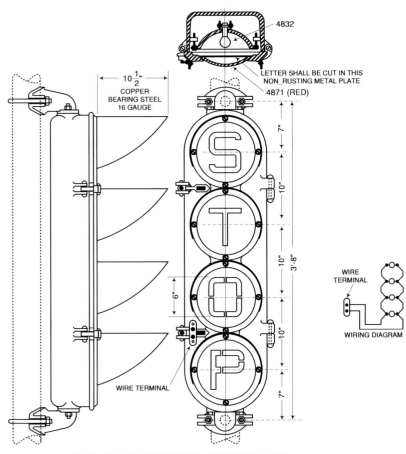

4653 ILLUMINATED STOP SIGN COMPLETE

4832

LETTER SHALL BE CUT IN THIS
NON_RUSTING METAL PLATE
4871 (RED)

COPPER
BEARING STEEL
16 GAUGE

10 1/2"

7"

10"

10"

3'-8"

6"

10"

7"

WIRE TERMINAL

WIRE TERMINAL

WIRING DIAGRAM

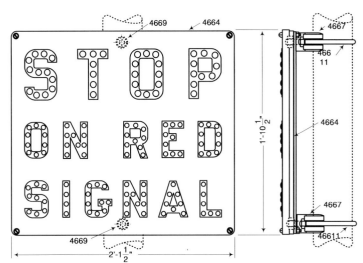

4652 REFLECTOR STOP ON RED SIGNAL SIGN

COMPLETE
A.R.A. MANUAL 1933

4669   4664

4666
11

4664

4667

4667

46611

4669

4669

2'-1 1/2"

1'-10 1/2"

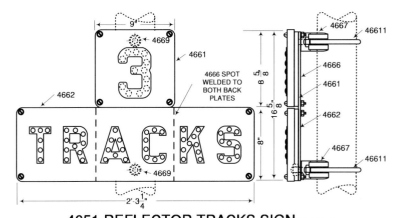

4651 REFLECTOR TRACKS SIGN COMPLETE

SPECIFY NUMERAL REQUIRED ON REQUISITION
A.R.A. MANUAL 1933

9"

4669

4661

4666 SPOT
WELDED TO
BOTH BACK
PLATES

4662

4669

4667

46611

4666

4661

4662

4667

46611

2'-3 1/4"

8"

16 5/8"

5 5/8"

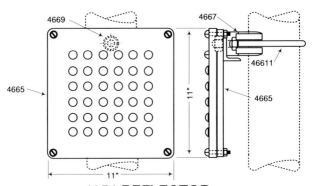

**4654 REFLECTOR
CROSSING SIGNAL MARKER**

A.R.A. MANUAL 1933   COMPLETE

4669

4667

46611

4665

4665

11"

11"

NOTE:-
1. WHERE NO DETAIL REFERENCE IS GIVEN, THE MANUFACTURER'S
   STANDARD APPARATUS SHALL BE FURNISHED.
2. SIGN 4653 SHALL BE WIRED IN ACCORDANCE WITH DIAGRAM
   SHOWN.
3. LIGHT UNITS OF SIGN 4653 SHALL BE EQUIPPED WITH INSULATED
   RECEPTACLES FOR SINGLE CONTACT BAYONET CANDELABRA
   BASES AND WIRE TERMINAL.
4. FOR CONTROL CIRCUITS FOR SIGN 4653 SEE PLAN No. S-860.
5. UNLESS OTHERWISE SPECIFIED, SIGNS SHALL BE FURNISHED
   ASSEMBLED COMPLETE WITH ALL PARTS FOR ATTACHING TO 4"
   O.D. PIPE POST.
6. FOR APPLICATION OF SIGNS SEE PLAN No. 66207.
7. FOR SPECIFICATIONS FOR REFLECTOR BUTTONS SEE PLAN S-467.
8. FOR DETAILS OF REFLECTOR SIGNS SEE PLAN S-466

THE PENNSYLVANIA RAILROAD
STANDARD
SIGNS
ILLUMINATED AND REFLECTING
FOR HIGHWAY CROSSINGS
STANDARD S-465-B, OCTOBER 1933

Redrawn from original PRR drawings by Jeff Scherb

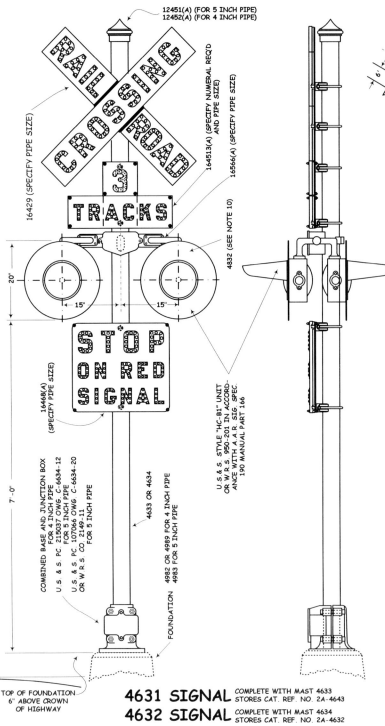

12451(A) (FOR 5 INCH PIPE)
12452(A) (FOR 4 INCH PIPE)

16429 (SPECIFY PIPE SIZE)

164513(A) (SPECIFY NUMERAL REQ'D AND PIPE SIZE)

16566(A) (SPECIFY PIPE SIZE)

4832 (SEE NOTE 10)

3 TRACKS

RAIL ROAD CROSSING

STOP ON RED SIGNAL

16468(A) (SPECIFY PIPE SIZE)

20"

15"   15"

7'-0"

COMBINED BASE AND JUNCTION BOX
FOR 4 INCH PIPE
U.S. & S. P.C. 215037 OWG. C-6634-12
FOR 5 INCH PIPE
U.S. & S. P.C. 107066 OWG. C-6634-20
OR W.R.S. CO 2149-11
FOR 5 INCH PIPE

4633 OR 4634

4982 OR 4989 FOR 4 INCH PIPE
4983 FOR 5 INCH PIPE

FOUNDATION

U.S. & S. STYLE "HC-B1" UNIT
OR W.R.S. 950-201 IN ACCORD-
ANCE WITH A.A.R. SIG. SPEC.
190 MANUAL PART 166

TOP OF FOUNDATION
6" ABOVE CROWN
OF HIGHWAY

4631 SIGNAL COMPLETE WITH MAST 4633
STORES CAT. REF. NO. 2A-4643

4632 SIGNAL COMPLETE WITH MAST 4634
STORES CAT. REF. NO. 2A-4632

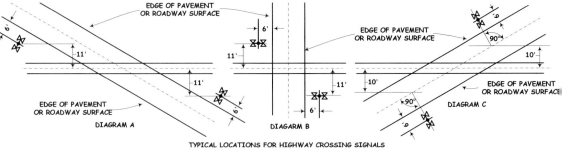

EDGE OF PAVEMENT OR ROADWAY SURFACE

6'

11'

11'

EDGE OF PAVEMENT OR ROADWAY SURFACE

DIAGRAM A

6'

DIAGARM B

6'

11'

11'

EDGE OF PAVEMENT OR ROADWAY SURFACE

90°

6'

10'

10'

EDGE OF PAVEMENT OR ROADWAY SURFACE

90°

6'

DIAGRAM C

TYPICAL LOCATIONS FOR HIGHWAY CROSSING SIGNALS

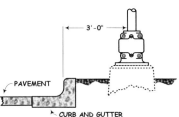

3'-0"

PAVEMENT

CURB AND GUTTER

DETAIL FOR CURB AND GUTTER LOCATIONS

NOTES:-
1. UNLESS OTHERWISE ORDERED, FLASHING LIGHT SIGNALS SHALL BE MOUNTED ON SAME MAST AS CROSSING SIGN (CROSSBUCK), BEING LOCATED IN ACCORDANCE WITH NOTE 13.
2. CROSSING SIGNS AS INDICATED, SHALL BE STANDARD "STOP" SIGN A.A.R. SIG. SEC. DRAWING 1654 IN LIEU OF "STOP ON RED SIGNAL" SIGNS AND OTHER SIGNS MAY BE IN-STALLED ONLY WHEN REQUIRED BY LOCAL OR STATE AUTHORITIES.
3. WHERE ONLY ONE TRACK CROSSES A HIGHWAY, THE "NUMBER OF TRACKS" 164513 SHALL BE REQUIRED ONLY WHEN REQUIRED BY LOCAL OR STATE AUTHORITIES.
4. PROVIDE PHANKILL SHIELDS IN "HC-B1" UNITS IF NECESSARY.
5. PARTS MARKED (A) REFER TO CURRENT ISSUE OF A.A.R. SIG. SEC. DRAWINGS
6. ONE HIGHWAY CROSSING BELL, LOCATED ON TOP OF MAST SHALL BE INSTALLED AT EACH CROSSING IF DESIRED, OR IF REQUIRED BY LOCAL OR STATE AUTHORITIES.
7. FOR NEW WORK, CONSIDERATION SHOULD BE GIVEN TO THE FUTURE ADDITION OF AUTOMATIC CROSSING GATES. IF GATES ARE TO BE ADDED, MAST 4634 WITH PROPER BASE AND FOUNDATION SHALL BE INSTALLED.
8. FOUNDATIONS WITH FOUNDATION BOLTS SHALL BE ORDERED SEPARATELY.
9. FOR TYPICAL CONTROL CIRCUITS SEE DRAWING S-860.
10. USE LAMP 4832 AS STANDARD. IF BETTER ILLUMINATION IS REQUIRED, USE 10 VOLT, 18 WATT LAMP U.S.& S. P.C. 151138 WITH CIRCUITS ARRANGED TO PROVIDE 9.0 TO 9.5 VOLTS AT LAMP.
11. SIGNALS SHALL NOT BE LIGHTED EXCEPT FOR AN APPROACHING TRAIN, THE RED LIGHTS FLASH ALTERNATELY 30 TO 45 TIMES PER MINUTE MUST BE DISPLAYED UNTIL TRAIN CLEARS THE CROSSING.
12. ALL MACHINE SCREWS, WASHERS, HINGE PINS, COTTER PINS, ETC. EXPOSED TO THE WEATHER SHALL BE OF NON-CORROSIVE METAL, OR CADMIUM PLATED. BACKGROUNDS AND HOODS SHALL BE MADE OF COPPER-BEARING STEEL.
13. DIAGRAMS A, B & C INDICATE TYPICAL LOCATIONS FOR SIGNALS, ACTUAL LOCATIONS ARE DETERMINED BY CONDITIONS IN THE FIELD.
14. PAINTING SHALL BE IN ACCORDANCE WITH A.A.R. SIG. SEC. SPEC. 120 MANUAL PART 110. FRONT EXPOSED PORTIONS OF LIGHT UNITS, HOODS AND BACKGROUNDS SHALL BE PAINTED WITH A FINISH COAT OF DULL BLACK S.C.R. 47-2020 OR 47-3208. ALL OTHER PARTS SHALL BE PAINTED WITH ALUMINUM.
15. AFTER INSTALLATION, ALL FOUNDATION BOLT HOLES IN BASE SHALL BE FILLED WITH NO-OX-ID COMPOUND.
16. IF SOIL CONDITIONS REQUIRE A DEEPER FOUNDATION, AN EXTRA FILLER BLOCK MAY BE ADDED, USING LONGER ANCHOR BOLTS.

LIGHT BEAMS
FRONT AND BACK LIGHT SHALL BE PROVIDED WITH 30° HORIZONTAL SPREAD AND 15° DOWNWARD DEFLECTIONS COVER GLASS. FOR UNUSUAL FIELD CONDITIONS SPECIAL LENS COMBINATIONS MAY BE OBTAINED.

THE PENNSYLVANIA RAILROAD
STANDARD
SIGNAL
FLASHING LIGHT HIGHWAY CROSSINGS

STANDARD S-4653E, FEBRUARY 1952

Redrawn from original PRR drawings by Jeff Scherb

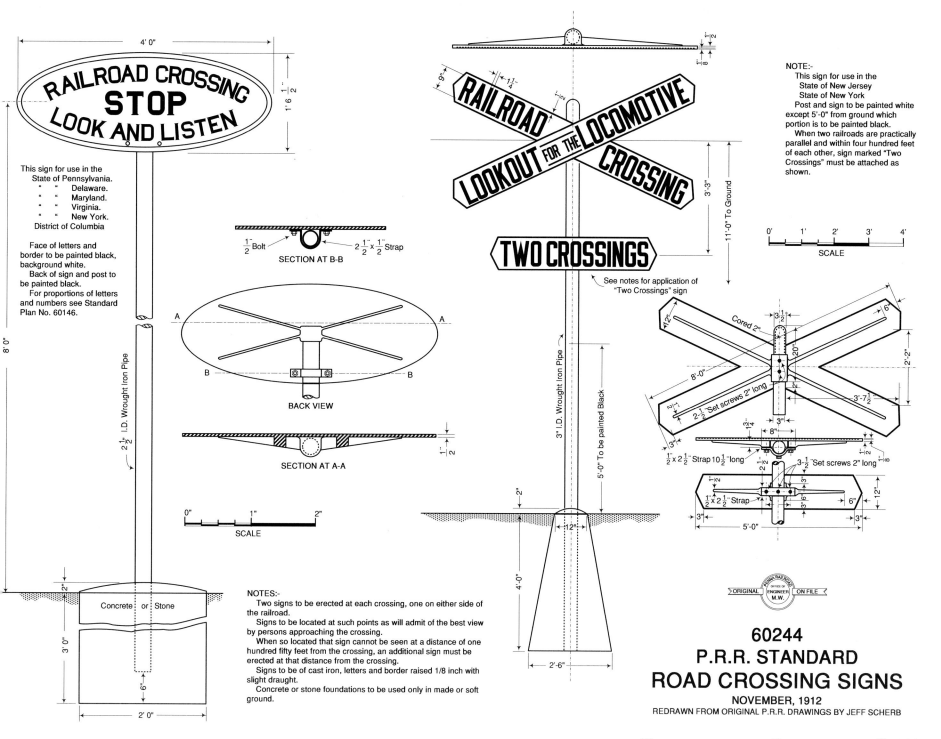

RAILROAD CROSSING
STOP
LOOK AND LISTEN

4' 0"

1' 6 ½"

8' 0"

This sign for use in the
State of Pennsylvania.
"   "   Delaware.
"   "   Maryland.
"   "   Virginia.
"   "   New York.
District of Columbia

Face of letters and
border to be painted black,
background white.
Back of sign and post to
be painted black.
For proportions of letters
and numbers see Standard
Plan No. 60146.

2 ½" I.D. Wrought Iron Pipe

2"

Concrete or Stone

3' 0"

6"

2' 0"

SECTION AT B-B

½" Bolt

2 ½" x ½" Strap

½"

A   A

B   B

BACK VIEW

SECTION AT A-A

½"

0"   1"   2"

SCALE

RAILROAD
LOOKOUT FOR THE LOCOMOTIVE
CROSSING

9"

1 1¼"

½"

TWO CROSSINGS

See notes for application of
"Two Crossings" sign

3' 3"

11'-0" To Ground

3" I.D. Wrought Iron Pipe

5'-0" To be painted Black

2"

4'-0"

12"

2'-6"

NOTES:-
    Two signs to be erected at each crossing, one on either side of
the railroad.
    Signs to be located at such points as will admit of the best view
by persons approaching the crossing.
    When so located that sign cannot be seen at a distance of one
hundred fifty feet from the crossing, an additional sign must be
erected at that distance from the crossing.
    Signs to be of cast iron, letters and border raised 1/8 inch with
slight draught.
    Concrete or stone foundations to be used only in made or soft
ground.

NOTE:-
    This sign for use in the
    State of New Jersey
    State of New York
    Post and sign to be painted white
except 5'-0" from ground which
portion is to be painted black.
    When two railroads are practically
parallel and within four hundred feet
of each other, sign marked "Two
Crossings" must be attached as
shown.

0'   1'   2'   3'   4'

SCALE

12"

Cored 2"

3 ½"

6"

20"

8'-0"

2'-2"

2 ½" Set screws 2" long

3'-7 ½"

3"

½"

3"

½" x 2 ½" Strap 10 ½" long

8"

3 ¼"

3-½" Set screws 2" long

½" x 2 ½" Strap

6"

12"

3"   5'-0"   3"

ORIGINAL ENGINEER ON FILE
M.W.

60244
P.R.R. STANDARD
ROAD CROSSING SIGNS
NOVEMBER, 1912
REDRAWN FROM ORIGINAL P.R.R. DRAWINGS BY JEFF SCHERB

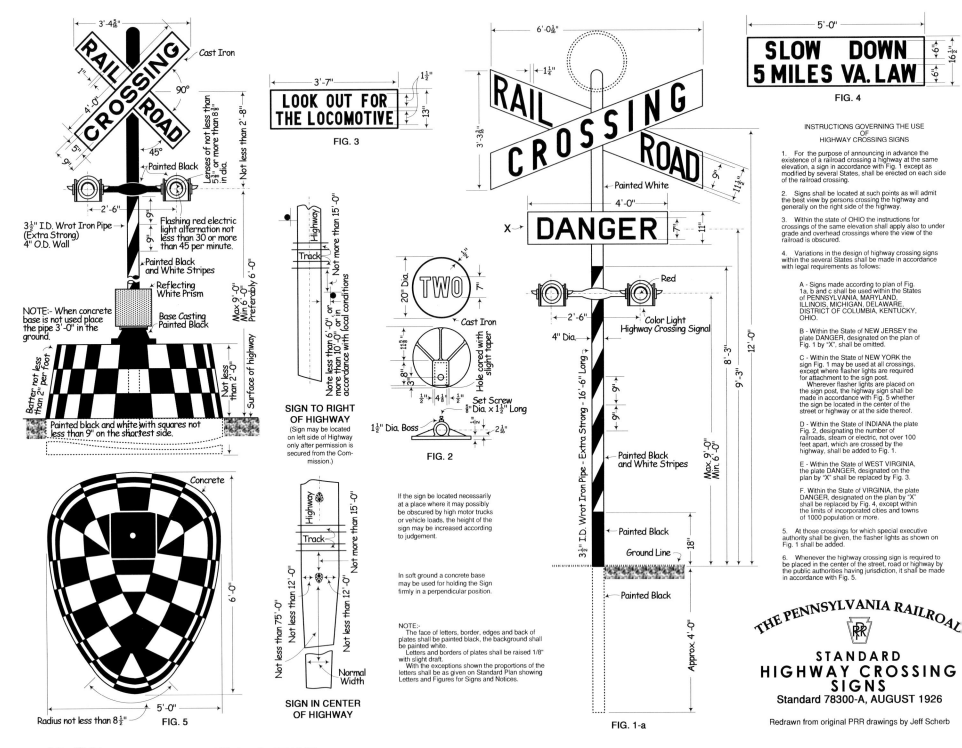

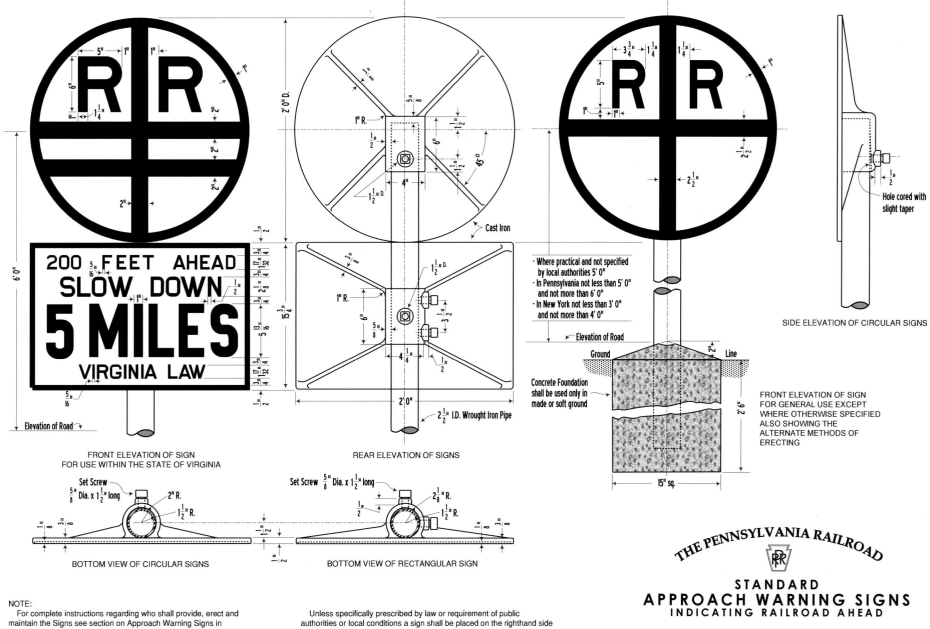

200 5/16 FEET AHEAD
SLOW DOWN
5 MILES
VIRGINIA LAW

Elevation of Road

FRONT ELEVATION OF SIGN
FOR USE WITHIN THE STATE OF VIRGINIA

Cast Iron

2 1/2" I.D. Wrought Iron Pipe

REAR ELEVATION OF SIGNS

· Where practical and not specified
  by local authorities 5' 0"
· In Pennsylvania not less than 5' 0"
  and not more than 6' 0"
· In New York not less than 3' 0"
  and not more than 4' 0"

Elevation of Road

Ground   Line

Concrete Foundation
shall be used only in
made or soft ground

15" sq.

FRONT ELEVATION OF SIGN
FOR GENERAL USE EXCEPT
WHERE OTHERWISE SPECIFIED
ALSO SHOWING THE
ALTERNATE METHODS OF
ERECTING

Hole cored with
slight taper

SIDE ELEVATION OF CIRCULAR SIGNS

Set Screw
5/8" Dia. x 1 1/2" long
2" R.
1 1/2" R.

BOTTOM VIEW OF CIRCULAR SIGNS

Set Screw 5/8" Dia. x 1 1/2" long
2 1/8" R.
1 1/2" R.

BOTTOM VIEW OF RECTANGULAR SIGN

NOTE:
For complete instructions regarding who shall provide, erect and maintain the Signs see section on Approach Warning Signs in Specifications for Standard Track Construction No. C.E. 78 (basic number)
Letters, figures, cross bars and borders shall be raised 1/8 inch with slight draft and shall be painted black with a white background, the edges and back of signs and the pipe shall be painted black.

Unless specifically prescribed by law or requirement of public authorities or local conditions a sign shall be placed on the righthand side of the highway, at a distance of 300 feet in either direction from the intersection of the highway and the railroad.
Requisition form must specify length of pipe required.

THE PENNSYLVANIA RAILROAD

PRR

STANDARD
APPROACH WARNING SIGNS
INDICATING RAILROAD AHEAD

Standard 78310-B, JUNE, 1930

Redrawn from original PRR drawings by Jeff Scherb

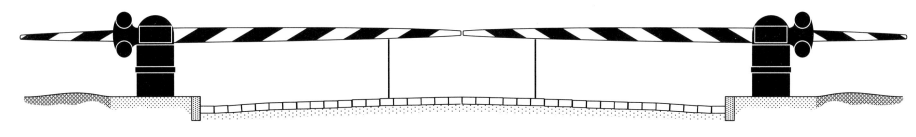

NOTE:
Both sides of the gates shall be painted as shown; mechanism housings and counter weights, painted black.

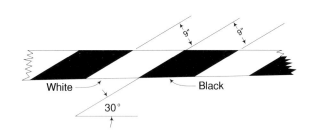

White — Black

30°

PENNSYLVANIA SYSTEM

STANDARD
PAINTING FOR HIGHWAY CROSSING GATES
STANDARD #78320-A, 1921

Redrawn from original PRR drawings by Jeff Scherb

NOTE:
 Disc shall be made of metal with edge rolled or folded.
 Letters shall be 5 inches high, 3 inches wide and 3/4 inch stroke.
 Letters, border and handle shall be painted Black, background White.
 Both sides of disc the same.

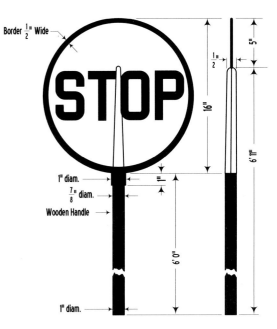

Border $\frac{1}{2}$" Wide

STOP

$\frac{1}{2}$"
5"
16"
6'11"

1" diam.
$\frac{7}{8}$" diam.
Wooden Handle
6'0"

1" diam.

PENNSYLVANIA SYSTEM
STANDARD
STOP SIGN
FOR GRADE CROSSING WATCHMEN
STANDARD #78315-A, JUNE 1930
Redrawn from original PRR drawings
by Jeff Scherb

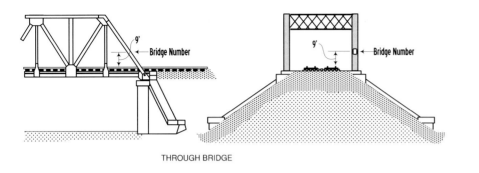

THROUGH BRIDGE

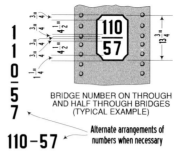

BRIDGE NUMBER ON THROUGH
AND HALF THROUGH BRIDGES
(TYPICAL EXAMPLE)

110–57

Alternate arrangements of
numbers when necessary

HALF THROUGH BRIDGE

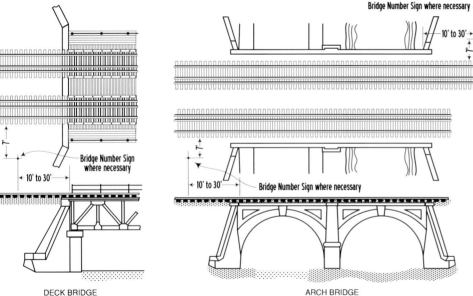

DECK BRIDGE

ARCH BRIDGE

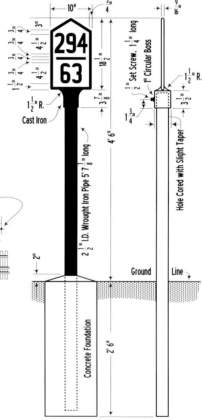

BRIDGE NUMBER SIGN
(TYPICAL EXAMPLE)

NOTE:

A bridge number must be given to a structure of any character carrying the roadway fill or tracks over an opening of 5 feet or more in width or diameter. The bridge number is made up of two parts, the first being the number of the preceding mile post (numbered from the basic zero point) and the second part being the distance in hundredths of a mile beyond said mile post to the center line of the bridge.

In all cases, where possible, the bridge numbers shall be placed so that they will be legible from the front or rear ends of a train, and may be painted either on the back wall, abutment, wing wall, end of truss, approach or end of half-through girder.

One number at least shall be placed on all bridges or structures.

If the numbers cannot be located as prescribed in second paragraph, main line bridges of less than 100 feet in length and all bridges on large branch lines shall have one Bridge Number Sign. On main line bridges 100 feet of more in length two numbers or two Bridge Number Signs shall be used.

On bridges on small branch lines where the number cannot be located as prescribed in second paragraph, it shall be painted just above or below painting date if it be a metal bridge, or on the side of any other structure where it may be readily seen.

Where one number only is used for a bridge, it shall be located on the right hand side of the roadway going north or west.

Where two numbers are used for a bridge, one is located as above and the other diagonally opposite at the other end of the bridge.

Where more economical to do so and clearance will permit, Bridge Number Sign may be set on parapet wall or back wall of the bridge.

A bridge number sign painted on a bridge shall be black on a white background.

A Bridge Number sign shall have all parts painted black except the background which shall be white, the figures and border appear on both sides of the sign and the border raised 1/8 inch with slight draft.

Figures shall be of the proportions as shown in Standard Plan of Letters and Figures for Signs and Notices, basic number 78000.

Concrete foundation shall be used only in made or soft ground.

A bridge number must also be given to a bridge structure of any character crossing over the railroad and shall be determined as prescribed above. The numbers shall be placed on a pier or the abutments or in some other conspicuous location so that they will be legible from the front and rear ends of a train passing under the bridge, and otherwise conform to the instructions given for track bridges.

PENNSYLVANIA SYSTEM

STANDARD
METHOD OF NUMBERING BRIDGES
AND
BRIDGE NUMBER SIGN

Standard #78500-B, October, 1921

Redrawn from original PRR drawings by Jeff Scherb

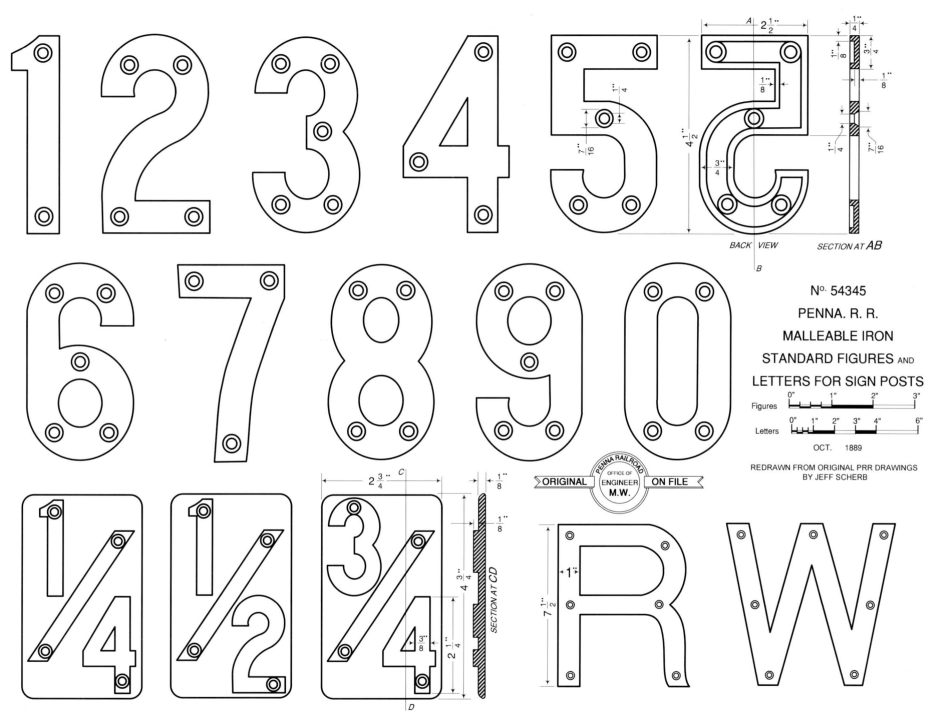

No. 54345

PENNA. R. R.

MALLEABLE IRON

STANDARD FIGURES AND

LETTERS FOR SIGN POSTS

OCT. 1889

REDRAWN FROM ORIGINAL PRR DRAWINGS
BY JEFF SCHERB

BACK VIEW   SECTION AT AB

SECTION AT CD

Putting it all together on a model railroad

THE MATERIAL IN THIS BOOK can provide the modeler with a comprehensive guide to superdetailing a model railroad right-of-way. In planning a detailed and prototypical right-of-way, there are several places to start. If a goal of the layout is prototypical operation, then consider the trackside elements early in the trackplanning phase. For example, unmanned Block Limits require stops to contact the dispatcher for permission to proceed. If a dummy or operational signal system is to be part of the layout, consider the placement of signal towers and interlocking towers. For a realistic signal system, Oregon Rail Supply makes position-light signal kits and signal heads that match the Pennsylvania standard.

Passenger operation can be greatly enhanced at little cost of space by adding small passenger shelters, which don't require the presence (or suggestion) of a town large enough to support the construction of a full station. If the layout is to be set in the steam era, be sure to consider the location of water tanks to service thirsty steam engines.

Consider how mile posts might be used to simulate distance — plan for these as well as section and division posts if the layout is large enough. The mile posts should be placed sequentially, but don't necessarily have to be consecutive — skipping consecutive numbers can be another way to enhance the illusion of distance.

If scenic realism is also a goal, once the basic trackplan is nearly complete and scenic elements are being planned, consider the placement of crossings, tool sheds and other small structures. Carefully consider the location of culverts. Seldom modeled, culverts are a necessity on the prototype to prevent drainage water from rainstorms and spring thaws from washing over the tracks. Imagine a heavy rain washing over your scenery — where would the water go? These are best planned along with the contours of the scenery, and it is always easiest to provide breaks in the roadbed for culverts before the track is laid.

Along the main, find locations for signal towers — in the latter part of the 19th century and into the 20th, these towers were placed every few miles along busy lines. In locations where Block Limits are to be placed, make sure a phone box or telephone booth is present to allow the engineer to call the dispatcher.

If the era modeled is pre-WWII, busy grade crossings should be protected by a watchman, which requires a watchman's shed. A stop sign leaning up against a watch box makes a great detail.

There are numerous opportunities for trackside signs on the layout. Wherever there is a grade crossing, whistle posts should appear. Prototype placement would be approximately 1/4 mile from the crossing, but for model purposes, this can be compressed to 200 scale feet or less. Similarly, ring signs can be placed 50 scale feet from stations. Flanger signs can be placed 50 scale feet from grade crossings, switches, bridges and other trackage that requires the lifting of the flanger blade.

Most of the details described above fall into the "one evening" category, and all can greatly enhance the realism of the scene. Many of them can add interesting aspects to model railroad operations. It's this type of detail that really sets a layout apart from the rest. ▰

ABOUT THE DRAWINGS

FEW EXAMPLES of the subjects in this book remain, so the drawings in this volume were mostly redrawn from original Pennsylvania Railroad Standard Plans, photographs and other sources. Every attempt has been made to ensure that the drawings are accurate renditions of the prototypes, but from time to time some interpretation was required since the original drawings weren't always scaled or dimensioned as accurately as they might be had they been drawn today with modern computer-aided-drafting software.

In the case of drawings made from old photographs, dimensions were scaled from one or more known or easily determinable dimensions, so again, while every attempt toward accuracy has been made, it is likely that some minor deviations from exact prototype dimensions have crept into the drawings.

An attempt has been made to match the character of the original hand lettering of the drawings with currently available fonts — mostly Helvetica, Comic Sans and Blue Highway Condensed fonts were used for this purpose.

All of the drawings were produced with Microsoft Visio 2002 on an IBM Thinkpad 240x notebook computer running Windows 2000 Professional.

The drawings in this volume are copyrighted by the author, and may be reproduced by individuals for non-commercial use only. Permission for any other use must be obtained in advance from the author and publisher. ▼